RED H

For a complete list of books in this series, see the back of this book.

Red Hot + Blue

John S. Garrison

BLOOMSBURY ACADEMIC
NEW YORK • LONDON • OXFORD • NEW DELHI • SYDNEY

BLOOMSBURY ACADEMIC
Bloomsbury Publishing Inc
1385 Broadway, New York, NY 10018, USA
50 Bedford Square, London, WC1B 3DP, UK
29 Earlsfort Terrace, Dublin 2, Ireland

BLOOMSBURY, BLOOMSBURY ACADEMIC and the Diana logo are
trademarks of Bloomsbury Publishing Plc

First published in the United States of America 2024

Bloomsbury Publishing Inc does not have any control over, or
responsibility for, any third-party websites referred to or in this book.
All internet addresses given in this book were correct at the time of
going to press. The author and publisher regret any inconvenience
caused if addresses have changed or sites have ceased to exist, but can
accept no responsibility for any such changes.

Whilst every effort has been made to locate copyright holders
the publishers would be grateful to hear from any person(s) not
here acknowledged.

A catalog record for this book is available from the Library of Congress.

ISBN: PB: 979-8-7651-0663-1
        ePDF: 979-8-7651-0665-5
        eBook: 979-8-7651-0664-8

Series: 33 1/3

Typeset by Integra Software Services Pvt. Ltd.
Printed and bound in Great Britain

To find out more about our authors and books visit www.bloomsbury.
com and sign up for our newsletters.

Contents

Images

Author's Note

As I discuss throughout this book, *Red Hot + Blue* was more than a music album. It was a cultural event. Its release coincided with a primetime television special shown in thirty countries, involved contributions by well-known artists, and supported a public education campaign. To obtain a full sense of the scope of the project, you may wish to view these elements as you read the book. They are available at the website: https://redhot.org/project/red-hot-blue/. And, of course, first and foremost give this album a listen and a re-listen. Watch the videos. And be transported not just back to 1990 but to Porter's era as well.

Introduction: Something for the Boys*

It's Saturday evening, July 8, 1995. I'm attending a special performance by the San Francisco Gay Men's Chorus called "Swellegant Elegance: The Life and Music of Cole Porter." I'm with my friend David, who has also recently moved to San Francisco. We share an apartment just a few blocks off Castro Street. My mom is with us, and she has recently launched a new local chapter of PFLAG (Parents, Families, and Friends of Lesbians and Gays) in the suburb where I grew up. Tonight is just a pinprick in my personal history, but it will become a flashbulb memory to which I will return many times. The snapshot, once unfolded, captures the evocative questions that I've since pursued in my subsequent career of writing about queer lives of the past. That night, I've only recently

*I draw the title of this chapter from Porter's work, as I do all the chapter and section-header titles. This 1943 musical starred Ethel Merman, with a book by Herbert and Dorothy Fields. *Something for the Boys* played both on Broadway and in the West End in addition to a national tour. It depicts a burlesque queen, a carnival hawker, and defense worker who take over a Texas ranch and turn it into a boarding house for soldiers' wives.

graduated from college, but I would eventually write several books that trace the cultural history of love and desire. And this particular evening showcases why *Red Hot + Blue* might offer if not an origin story then certainly a way-marker for my path toward my intellectual interests. The album offers a case study that intertwines an array of histories: my own, Cole Porter's, and that of HIV/AIDS as well as the music industry's response to the epidemic.

To be honest, I'm not sure if I knew about *Red Hot + Blue* in 1995. The album was released in 1990, but I don't think I owned a copy until after I attended that concert. Today, when I look over the tracklist, it reads like an inventory of many of my favorite artists at that time: Aaron Neville, Debbie Harry, Fine Young Cannibals, k.d. lang, Thompson Twins, and so many others. Today, when I watch the music videos, I recognize scenes from MTV or VH-1 channel surfing: Bono with U2 on a rooftop staircase at night, Sinéad O'Connor wearing a blonde wig while she croons in an old-timey dancehall, Annie Lennox watching home movies of a small child playing on the beach. So I must have been aware of the album's contents even if I didn't know about it as a major fundraising effort with a groundbreaking primetime television special. And, I think no one could have known how *Red Hot + Blue* would come to signify a turning point in the music industry's response to the epidemic.

To reacquaint myself with the album today is to send a depth-charge into the past and let memory surge to the surface of *the now*. Indeed, I find that I can only write about this particular past in the present tense. To talk about *Red Hot + Blue* is to re-immerse myself in a half-forgotten cultural moment. And to recover that album now is to recover my own memories of that time: the 1980s when I became aware of AIDS in high school and the 1990s when I came out as a young gay man, joining a community haunted by disease and encumbered with loss. The album itself for me is an *archive of feelings*, to borrow the title of Ann Cvetkovich's wonderful book on queer history. The album for me is a well of memory.

But here, now, I'm still in that evening. I'm still listening to the Chorus sing Cole Porter. And that's not all I'm hearing. The event is hosted by Harvey Fierstein, who relates vignettes of Porter's life in between the songs. I can't see Fierstein too clearly, both because we're sitting far away from the stage and because I can't picture him as a man thirty years younger than the one I've seen on television recently. But I do clearly recall the raspy voice which I knew from his role as the drag performer at the center of *Torch Song Trilogy*, the 1988 film which also starred Anne Bancroft as his disapproving mother and Matthew Broderick as his lover who is beaten to death in a homophobic attack. So, we're hearing about Cole's time at Yale writing football fight songs, then living the high life in Paris of the 1920s, and then falling in and out of love with his wife, with a dancer, with a soldier. And we're also hearing Porter's most famous songs—"Anything Goes," "Blow, Gabriel, Blow," "I Loved Him, but He Didn't Love Me," "My Heart Belongs to Daddy," and "You're the Top!"—as they become bawdy, campy, or soulful queer anthems.

The performance sparks a range of emotions among the members of the audience. There's a lot of laughter, of course. Porter is so brilliant with innuendo. The chorus members really lay into the refrain of his song about the horn-playing archangel: "Oh, blow, Gabriel, blow, / Go on and blow, Gabriel, blow!" Everyone seems to know exactly what Porter refers to when the lyrics of the next song say, "If, baby, I'm the bottom, you're the top!" So many of the songs seem coded as gay, even if some of the words in the lyrics didn't have sexual or queer connotations when Porter wrote them. It's freeing and it's joyful, but I have to admit to cringing a little (then during the performance and even now as I write) at the thought of my mom picturing gay sex. I mean, I know she knows about sex and knows that I have sex. But somehow I don't want us both picturing it at the same time.

And then there are the somber notes of the evening, for instance when "Every Time We Say Goodbye" resounds as an elegy to the many members of the Chorus who have been lost to AIDS. Songs like this one show how profoundly Porter knew what it was like to live a life constantly in the shadow of loss. He mourned like we're mourning that evening, even if Porter's life ended before the HIV epidemic started (1964 and 1981, respectively). When I hear that song, both on that night and as I compose this book, I wonder how much my mom was worrying at that moment about whether I'd become infected with the virus.

The performance resonates deeply with everyone in the audience—we're all caught up in the moment—but I think it especially resonates with those of us who are queer, moved by seeing ourselves reflected in the heart of American musical history. That's not to say it doesn't resonate with my mom and others who aren't gay. Many, maybe even most, of the people in the audience are ones who have queer people in their lives at the time or who are concerned about the

HIV/AIDS crisis. Indeed, as a PFLAG leader, my mom talked to lots of people whose families had rejected them or with lots of parents whose impulse was to reject the child they'd raised. I'm lucky to have parents who didn't skip a beat in accepting me, and who in fact bought the tickets for this very performance.

The blurring of past and present is so striking because we're hearing the familiar arrangements of the songs—perhaps known from albums like Ella Fitzgerald's *Songbook* series— sung by more than a hundred voices in unison. While the re-imagined versions on *Red Hot + Blue* are at-times striking in their originality, the Chorus tonight doesn't need to change the arrangements or the lyrics to make these songs about gay life or about loss in the wake of the AIDS epidemic. The way that the Chorus performs the songs of the past to celebrate our lives in the present strikes me as a powerful instance of how both personal histories and community histories are formed through music. This is what listening to music does, isn't it? It so often invites us to occupy multiple time periods at once: the time when we're listening, the time when we first heard the song, and the broader period when the song was written or performed. Music, and particularly these Cole Porter classics, summons not just feelings but also memories, personal ones as well as cultural ones.

When I think of that Saturday evening, it pulls me into a whirligig of time. I'm my younger self, filled with hope about how to make my own way in the world as my life unfolds while also wondering how I connect to a community with such a traumatic recent past. And I'm wanting to know more about how that community links to a larger history. Even today I yearn for a deeper understanding of that history. But in 1995 I'm in a moment very different from today. The evening's taking place before my mom had her stroke, before I'd begun to lose so many people I knew to AIDS. And it's just before the arrival of new antiviral treatments that would change the course of the epidemic.

A Picture of Me without You

I should say also that for all the ways in which that particular evening is so full—of music, of history, of beginnings—it's also an evening that renders visible the palpable presence of loss. The singers testify to the joy of their own survival all the while reminding us of how many people have been lost to AIDS. How could we even begin to imagine the weight of the loss experienced by those men on stage and the community they represent? How do they sing for those who are absent?

There is a photograph that answers these questions so poignantly (Figure. I.1). In 1993, the Chorus's artistic director Stan Hill conceives a startling way to portray the toll of the AIDS crisis. He stages a portrait of the Chorus with only seven of their members in white dress shirts, facing the audience. The rest of the chorus, all 117 of them, are dressed in black and facing away from the audience. The image's caption is nothing short of heartbreaking:

> The men in white are the surviving members of the original San Francisco Gay Men's Chorus. The others represent those lost to AIDS.

Figure I.1 The San Francisco Gay Men's Chorus, May 1993, demonstrating the impact of AIDS on the members of the chorus. (Photo by Eric Luse/San Francisco Chronicle via Getty Images).

In 1996, the same picture is rereleased with this sentence added:

> Today, all their backs would be turned because the obituary list is now 47 names longer than the chorus roster. For each man singing these days, more than one chorus member has died of AIDS.

In December of 2020, the Chorus posted that picture from 1993 on their Facebook page with the caption:

> The Chorus has lost over 300 members to HIV/AIDS since 1981, and we sing for them each time we take the stage.

I think this comment uniquely helps us think about how music is a tie to the past. Each time a Cole Porter song is performed, even for the thousandth or hundred-thousandth time, it resuscitates his voice in the sense that he was first to sing it at his piano or with pencil in hand. For the Chorus on that night, each voice intermingles the singer's individual feelings, the cultural memory of Porter, and the collective memory of the Chorus that mourns its lost members. So even the happy songs are songs of mourning for a lost composer, lost singers, and lost opportunities for joy. Even just writing that sentence, I'm not sure whether to feel sad or happy, wistful or hopeful. But I do know that the virus imbued the early 1990s with such sheer precarity. I remember feeling like each time a favorite song filled the dance floor or came on the radio, it took on a particular serendipity. Maybe all young people experience music that way, but for me the epidemic made a difference. I remember feeling like the next time I saw a friend, he might tell me that someone we knew had died or that he had learned he was HIV-positive. Or I might have learned since our last meeting that I had been infected. That made every song I heard and every goodbye I said charged with more meaning, more intensity.

Gosh, that made every time feel a little like dying.

Red Hot and Blue

In some ways, I think I should have known about *Red Hot + Blue* when it was released in 1990. But my mind was occupied with other things: moving away from home, starting college, and desperately hiding the fact that I might be, could be, or didn't want anyone to possibly think that I was gay. A few years later, I'd be out and I'd be lucky to have a family that was not only accepting but also ready to lead support groups, argue with their church leaders, and march in Pride parades. *Red Hot + Blue* was a reaction to a world colder and harsher than the producers wanted the world to be. It was created in response to the frequently hostile world I would inherit, a world I was not fully aware that I was already living in. The album was *before my time* in a certain kind of way. Even though I was around when it was released, I wasn't ready to make sense of it. It might only be now, through the lens of retrospect, that I can begin to do so.

The AIDS epidemic begins in 1981, but the story of *Red Hot + Blue* begins in 1989. While many talented and passionate people would come together to bring the album into the world, it all starts with John Carlin. His early career involved writing about the art scene in New York and, through that, he had become friends with visual artists such as Keith Haring and David Wojnarowicz. Both of these artists used their talents to express their hope or rage about the epidemic, and both would die in the early 1990s from the disease. *Red Hot + Blue* was thus a passion-project for Carlin, and it was also a natural segue for him, given his training in art history and design. He has likened the work of creating this album (and the ensuing albums in the series from the Red Hot Organization) to "curating an exhibition" because "it's an art."[1] Such a comparison is a useful way to think about *Red Hot + Blue*. One can't discuss the songs without thinking about the music videos and the television special, as well as the visuals of the print campaign that accompanied these other elements.

Carlin would soon partner with filmmaker Leigh Blake and David Byrne, who was the first musical artist to come on board the project. To garner traction, *Red Hot + Blue* needed star power. And that came from both Blake's network in the music industry and from Byrne himself, who brought not only strong name recognition but also his own personal connection to the epidemic. His sister-in-law was HIV-positive at the time and would later die from the disease in 1992.[2]

I'm sure there were a lot of people who felt like new infections were happening all around them. And the experience those people were having was bumping up against a world where it seemed like so many people didn't know much about the disease and rarely thought about AIDS, except when there was an occasional mention on the news. 1990 was a year when the crisis was reaching new heights, and there was no end in sight. As Roxane Gay recalls,

> In the '90s, when we were all in ACT UP, I don't know that any of us thought the disease was going to be possible to overcome. [...] But all we did was go to funerals; it did feel like there was no hope[.] It was so bad—I think the next generation has no idea how bad it *actually* was.[3]

For some readers of this book, the early 1990s might feel like ancient history, either because it was only experienced by a previous generation or because the previous terror of the disease has been eclipsed by its status as manageable for many people. Today, pre-exposure prophylactic (PrEP) medications can protect people against infection. Today, effective treatments keep infected people healthy and make the virus undetectable (and thereby untransmittable to others). For so many people who were infected at the time of the album's release, though, these new treatments would come too late.

To understand the context of *Red Hot + Blue*, we need to place ourselves in this moment when things were so bad and seemed like they could only get worse. The virus was happening at home, and it was appearing in the headlines. Rock Hudson was revealed to be HIV-positive in 1985, Magic Johnson in 1991, Freddie Mercury in 1991, and Arthur Ashe in 1992. Ryan White became infected in 1984 and died in 1990. It was only the luck of timing that Johnson would remain healthy long enough to have access to the combination therapies that would arrive in the mid-1990s. For him, HIV would become a chronic condition with which he might live a long life. It might be difficult to conceive of the shock it was to learn that a celebrity was HIV-positive in the early 1990s. When Charlie Sheen announced that he was HIV-positive in 2015, it was hardly met with the shock level of, for example, the news about Robert Reed (who played the father on *The Brady Bunch*) having AIDS in 1992. Such a diagnosis is no longer a death sentence or a likely indicator of shamefully hidden gay identity.

In the early nineties, there was no end in sight to the pandemic. Two years after *Red Hot + Blue* was released, AIDS would become the number-one cause of death for US men aged twenty-five to forty-four. In 1994, the disease would be the leading cause of death for all Americans in that age group.

The pandemic would reach its peak in 1995, just before the introduction of those drug cocktails that would change its course. In 1990, funding was so desperately needed. And even more crucial was increased awareness of the disease and much more frank talk about how it was transmitted.

Carlin, Blake, and Byrne brought together some of the decade's hottest artists, and it marked a turning point in terms of how the music industry would respond to the AIDS epidemic. It was one of the first large-scale AIDS benefits in the music business, and it featured artists talking about a disease that had been met with so much stigma and so much silence. The album sold over a million copies worldwide and raised funds for AIDS organizations, including ACT UP, that were demanding more government funding for treatment and more access from pharmaceutical companies to the treatments that offered any kind of hope of extending the lives of people with HIV.[4]

Red Hot + Blue featured twenty songs by Cole Porter, and the album took its name from a 1936 Broadway musical, with music and lyrics by Porter and starring Ethel Merman and Bob Hope. Perhaps some of the early names attached to the project made sense. Andy Bell and Jimmy Somerville were both out. And perhaps there are some names that might seem conspicuously absent. Neither Madonna nor George Michael were available (and this was still a time when Michael was not publicly open about his sexuality), but both artists would become involved in future Red Hot albums. Many of the songs on the album are chestnuts for fans of blues, jazz, or musical theater; and many of the artists are icons of the 1980s and 1990s musical moment (Figure I.2).

Artist	Song
Neneh Cherry	"I've Got You under My Skin"
The Neville Brothers	"In the Still of the Night"
Sinéad O'Connor	"You Do Something to Me"
Salif Keita	"Begin the Beguine"
The Fine Young Cannibals	"Love for Sale"
Deborah Harry + Iggy Pop	"Well, Did You Evah!"
Kirsty MacColl + The Pogues	"Miss Otis Regrets/Just One of Those Things"
David Byrne	"Don't Fence Me In"
Tom Waits	"It's All Right With Me"
Annie Lenox	"Ev'ry Time We Say Goodbye"
U2	"Night+Day"
Les Négresses Vertes	"I Love Paris"
k.d. lang	"So in Love"
Thompson Twins	"Who Wants to be a Millionaire?"
Erasure	"Too Darn Hot"
The Jungle Brothers	"I Get a Kick Out of You"
Lisa Stansfield	"Down in the Depths"
Jimmy Somervile	"From This Moment On"
Jody Watley	"After You, Who?"
Aztec Camera	"Do I Love You?"

Figure I.2 Track list for *Red Hot + Blue*.

Even though the album featured very contemporary artists and tackled a very contemporary issue, the songs were from an earlier time: the heyday of the 1930s and 1940s when Porter's music was defining the jazz standard. This might seem an odd choice if the goal was to speak to the present moment. But these songs have the quality of being so memorable, even to those who might not recall having heard them. Porter's lyrics are so thoroughly diffused into the English language that they surely would have sounded familiar to many 1990s listeners as well as those today. As Adam Gopnik puts it in a 2020 *New Yorker* essay, "Almost inhumanly prolific, the songwriter produced a new kind of American lyric—and language."[5] And this curious combination of old and new struck a resonant chord with many reviewers. "Benefit projects, while long on good intentions, can be woefully short on artistic merit. That cannot be said of *Red Hot + Blue*," wrote the *Chicago Tribune*.[6]

When the *Red Hot + Blue* project was imagined, there had been no major multi-artist and multi-platform effort by the music industry to support the fight against AIDS. In 1986, there had been the release of the single "That's What Friends Are For," featuring Gladys Knight, Elton John, Dionne Warwick, and Stevie Wonder doing their own version of the Burt Bacharach and Carole Bayer Sager song. The single did raise $3M for the American Foundation for AIDS Research (AmFAR). I do remember being very moved by the song, not only because it was very good but because it was one of the earliest music videos I had seen. It won Grammy Awards for Best Pop Performance by a Duo or Group with Vocals and for Song of the Year. But, listening to the song now, I think I feel the same way I felt when I first heard it. It's a sad song. It's about mourning and it's about giving support, about being a caregiver. There is a deep bond between a caregiver and an ill person.[7] And there are deep bonds between people who become involved in social movements.[8] Friendship was a big part of the fight against AIDS, surely, but it was not enough.

Madonna had included an insert about HIV in her 1989 *Like a Prayer* album. I don't remember the insert, but I do remember *Truth or Dare* (1991), the film which captured her 1990 Blond Ambition world tour. And I do remember how, in the film, we hear her dedicate a concert to Keith Haring who had died the previous year and we see a moment of silence for those lost to AIDS during a Pride parade. Madonna's boldness about discussing sexuality in all its myriad expressions was a start, but she was also an outlier. Carlin remarks, "Given that this is an industry that sells sex to young people, I felt it had a moral responsibility to do more."[9] He was right. These early efforts needed to be groundwork for something bigger.

To talk about AIDS prevention, 1990s culture had to break through its taboos and get used to talking about sex. *Red Hot + Blue* wasn't alone. In 1990, Salt-n-Pepa's "Let's Talk About Sex" functioned as an anthem for those advocating honest speech, and in 1992 TLC wore condoms on their clothes.[10] Yet it was the scale of its endeavor that made *Red Hot + Blue* stand out as it was not just an album but also a television special which included music videos that tied the songs to themes of HIV transmission and treatment. It included brief public service announcement segments by Richard Gere and John Malkovich, as well as by clothing designer Jean-Paul Gaultier.

The program also featured artworks by Keith Haring, David Wojnarowicz, and the collective Gran Fury. As this book will describe, *Red Hot + Blue* thus capitalized on not just the way that music can *move us* but also the ways that music can serve the larger needs of a *movement.* Yet the album was also a look backward, a window into the life and work of Cole Porter who himself wrestled with the joy and sorrow that accompanies love in a judgmental society.

Another Sentimental Song

Red Hot + Blue offers a snapshot of distinctive yet overlapping periods of time. The album, like the Gay Chorus's "Swellegant Elegance," placed Cole Porter at the center of queer history, showcasing how his body of work reflected his life as a gay man—and could perfectly capture the lives of queer and disenfranchised people even half a century after he wrote the songs. In doing so, *Red Hot + Blue* reveals how we construct our histories through genealogies of music. And, in turn, it illuminates how music comes to feel as if it speaks to us personally and to the particular times in which we live.

I'm saying all of this with the clarity of 2024 and a position of having studied the history of gay people and the AIDS epidemic. But, as I think about *Red Hot + Blue* now, all of a sudden it's 1995. My mom's okay and the Chorus sings Cole Porter. And it's 1990 when a group of artists and music producers come together to help me even though I don't know the kind of help I'll need. And it's also 1981, when a new virus has been detected among homosexual men and I don't even know the word "homosexual."

Notes

1. Jim Farber, "Red Hot at 30: How Compilations Used Big Music Stars to Combat AIDS," *The Guardian* 25, 2020). Accessed October 19, 2023. https://www.theguardian.com/music/2020/sep/25/red-hot-at-30-aids-music

2. Farber, "Red Hot at 30."

3. Kurt Soller et al., "The 25 Most Influential Works of Postwar Queer Literature," *The New York Times* (June 22, 2023). https://www.nytimes.com/2023/06/22/t-magazine/queer-postwar-books-plays-poems.html

4. ACT UP is the "AIDS Coalition to Unleash Power," which was founded in 1987 as "a diverse, non-partisan group of individuals, united in anger and committed to direct action to end the AIDS crisis." There have been some excellent, recent histories of ACT UP's milestone activism, including Sarah Schulman's recent book *Let The Record Show: A Political History of ACT UP New York, 1987–1993* (New York: Macmillan, 2021) and the documentaries *United in Anger* (Dir. Jim Howard, The Ford Foundation, 2012) and *120 battements par minute (English: 120 BPM [Beats per Minute])* (Dir. Robin Campillo, Memento Films 1997). Another terrific resource is the ACT UP Oral History Project, an archive of 187 interviews with members of ACT UP New York. The project is located at https://actuporalhistory.org/ and is coordinated by Jim Hubbard and Sarah Schulman.

5. Adam Gopnik, "The Pleasure and Pain of Being Cole Porter," *New Yorker* (January 13, 2020).

6. Chris Heim, "*Red Hot + Blue* Benefit Album Shines," *Chicago Tribune* (December 14, 1990): O.

7. Caregivers themselves in the AIDS epidemic were often sexual minorities or racial minorities. Tom Roach has argued that the unique promises of friendship help us understand the deep bonds between people living with HIV and their caregivers; their "relation of shared estrangement" fosters social and political linkages between unlike individuals. Tom Roach, *Friendship as a Way of Life: Foucault, AIDS, and the Politics of Shared Estrangement* (Albany, NY: State University of New York Press, 2012), 41.

8. Interviewing queer women involved in ACT UP, Ann Cvetkovich observes how "friendship compensates for the unpleasant aspects of activism," such as sharing a jail cell or mourning the death of a fellow activist. Ann Cvetkovich, "AIDS Activism and Public Feelings: Documenting ACT UP's Lesbians," in *An Archive of Feelings: Trauma, Sexuality, and Lesbian Public Cultures* (Durham: Duke University Press, 2003), 173.

9. Qtd. in Farber, "Red Hot at 30: How Compilations Used Big Music Stars to Combat AIDS."

10. One version of Salt-n-Pepa's video featured a skeleton associated with the word "AIDS" and with a stamp saying "censored" in its mouth. Another version of the song called "Let's Talk About AIDS" got radio play and was included as a B-side on some singles of the song. In some ways, we might say that the *Red Hot + Blue* project responds to Salt-n-Pepa's bold call to action.

1

Let's Not Talk about Love

If you've heard any of the songs from *Red Hot + Blue,* it's probably U2's version of "Night and Day." It reached the #2 spot on Billboard's Modern Rock Tracks Chart, and it pioneered the denser, more industrial, and electronic sound that the band would explore in depth on *Achtung Baby* the following year. Not only was U2 one of the biggest names on the album but also this song was surely one of the most recognizable to listeners of any generation. Fred Astaire performed it first, in the 1932 musical *Gay Divorce.* Within three months of the show's opening, more than thirty artists had recorded the song. "Night and Day" has since been recorded by stars such as Bing Crosby, Ella Fitzgerald, Billie Holiday, Willie Nelson, Charlie Parker, Frank Sinatra, Ringo Starr, and Rod Stewart. With more than 100 versions having been recorded, it is the highest earner in the Porter catalog.[1]

Bono's engagement with *Red Hot + Blue* marks the beginning of his journey to becoming one of the most well-known AIDS spokespeople in the music industry, if not the world. As we will see throughout this book, the album was the start of something, inspiring musical artists not only to become involved in future Red Hot projects but also to become recognized advocates for HIV/AIDS funding and education on their own. Bono would go on to co-found "(RED)," an entity working with companies to raise money for HIV-related philanthropy. To date, (RED) has generated more than $465 million for HIV treatment and prevention in Africa through the Global Fund to Fight AIDS, Tuberculosis, and Malaria. The singer credits Leigh Blake for "bringing him into the movement in the first place."[2]

The music video for "Night and Day" was directed by German filmmaker Wim Wenders, whom viewers in 1990 might know from his films *Paris, Texas* (1984) and *Wings of Desire* (1987). In stark black-and-white, we first encounter the writing of the lyrics, as if they are a private entry in the singer's diary (Figure 1.1). We then find Bono shivering on a city rooftop, with the wind blowing through his hair and with his arms gripping his chest as he imagines holding an absent lover.

He may join a long lineage of singers to recount these words, but his performance emphasizes that the lyrics relate a story of loneliness and isolation.

The song is plaintive, a soulful expression of unfulfilled desire. The singer admits that the beloved is the only one for him, whether near to him or far. He thinks only of the beloved, night and day. His unheard cries strain to reach above the roaring, booming traffic as the absent beloved gets "under the hide of me/there's an oh, such a hungry yearning, burning inside of me." Hide. It's the strangest word in the song, but I think it's the most important one. On one level,

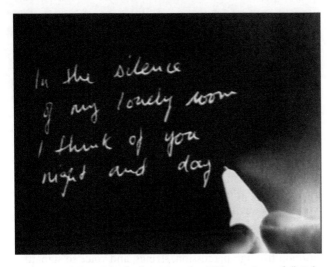

Figure 1.1 Wim Wenders's vision for U2's version of "Night and Day," screenshot from the music video.

it frames the singer's yearning as animalistic, as primal. On another level, the word "hide" emphasizes the hidden nature of their love affair. The more he thinks about the one he loves, the more the singer needs to hide it. And the more he hides it, the deeper he yearns. Listening to the song now as I write this, it's hard not to hear echoes of that other Porter classic, "I've Got You under My Skin." Both songs remind us that love can feel like something that invades us, that possesses us and that, well, infects us. Thinking about it this way, it's easy to understand why people in the time of Dante and

Shakespeare believed *love sickness* to be an actual physical ailment from which one suffered with little hope for a cure.

The emotion behind U2's rendition of "Night and Day" strikes me as authentic because I remember feeling such yearning in the early 1990s, during my early twenties. To hear the song now invokes not just an emotional memory but a bodily one too. That feeling of longing, of yearning, took me outside of myself. My body today may not be the exact same one I had when I was younger, but it still resonates with the memory of those feelings. My body recalls how it felt to be twenty-year-old me just as well as my mind does. At that age, my body was gripped by a desire to connect, one that was working its way into my hide just as I worked so feverishly to keep it hidden. And maybe the song strikes such a bodily chord because of U2's virtuoso ability to communicate raw emotion through percussion, strings, and voice so signature to their high period. Those early U2 songs capture so well the rattle of the constant promise that there is something wonderful in the distance waiting for you as well as the hum of satisfaction when one has a taste of that promise being fulfilled. One reviewer of *Red Hot + Blue* remarked that "Bono's strained, intense vocal helps turn the song into a pulsing rock anthem that has the same sense of urgency as the group's No. 1 hit 'With or Without You.'"[3] Another reviewer found U2 rendering the song so perfectly that it not only gives "us exactly what Porter wrote, but it gives us what Porter felt."[4]

Certainly, in "Night and Day," we can hear resonances of the type of longing that Porter expressed for one of the great loves of his life, Nelson Barclift. The two met in 1942 when the composer was working on the musical *Something for the Boys* and Barclift had just joined the US Army as the country entered the Second World War. So it was during the first year of the war when Cole sent the young soldier telegrams that said "Thinking of you constantly. All Love, Cole."[5] It was the thrill of early love, and thoughts about the absent Barclift were inspiring Porter to write songs such as "I'm In Love with a Soldier Boy" and "You'd Be Nice to Come Home To."[6] And it was in the wee hours of the night when Cole was composing those new songs. It was 2:30 a.m., and Cole was writing,

> It's bedtime […] so goodnight. I miss you like hell. Please don't forget me entirely. [B]e kind, Nelson, to someone who really is true-blue.[7]

Barclift was the one for him, but Porter could only yearn for him in his lonely room when they are simultaneously near and far.

The experience of desiring in private is an experience shared by those who have loved or been loved across history. But it became a deeply politicized experience—indeed, a matter of life and death—with the onset of the AIDS epidemic. And that's what makes U2's "Night and Day" all that more powerful. We don't need to look very far into the time period around 1990 when *Red Hot + Blue* was released in order to find these tensions expressed in raw form. The experimental film *Tongues Untied* (1989), directed and written by Marlon Riggs, gives voice to how marginalization intensifies feelings of isolation. Showcasing the voices of black men, for whom HIV infection rates were soaring all the while that prevention campaigns continued primarily to showcase white men, *Tongues Untied* reminds us how tensions around AIDS exacerbated other forms of prejudice. Even the briefest of snippets of dialogue from the film capture the complexity of the crossroads where silence, sexuality, and identity meet:

Voice One:	Silence is my shield.
Voice Two:	It crushes.
Voice One:	Silence is my cloak.
Voice Two:	It smothers.
Voice One:	Silence is my sword.
Voice Two:	It cuts both ways.[8]

To be out, to be outspoken, is to expose oneself, to be in danger. Yet to be out is to be free. The title of Porter's own romantic song, "Let's Not Talk about Love," captures perfectly how an injunction to avoid something can make the desire for it stronger. That's the attraction of taboo. Porter would never know a world where Riggs's film could be made. I remember *Tongues Untied* so well, though I don't think I saw it until after the film's director had died of AIDS in 1995.

Taken together, U2's "Night and Day" and this snippet from Riggs's film hint at the 1990s culture that demanded frank talk about love and the complexities of silence and desire. Indeed, they help us see why *Red Hot + Blue* was so desperately needed. The songs sing about love and loss, two seemingly private experiences, and make them necessarily public.

There's a sense of belatedness to which I find myself continually returning as I write this book. I discovered *Red*

Hot + Blue, Porter's queerness, and Riggs's film later than I wish I had. Perhaps belatedness is a shared experience for queer people, whose path often involves making sense of their sexual identities and locating their cultural history later than their straight counterparts. The AIDS crisis adds another later to this experience. I remember people during my early 20s, especially gay men I knew, expressing regret at being born too late to experience the world before AIDS. For many people with HIV in 1990, the treatments would come too late to help them. For many people, prevention information or an awareness that they themselves might be at risk for AIDS came too late. Like many governments around the world, the music industry was late to respond.

And I find myself wondering how many readers of this book may have been born too late to remember or to have lived through the height of the pandemic. And there are probably some whose attention was elsewhere in the early 1990s. For those of us who were tracking it so closely, the epidemic felt like the end of the world. But, for other people, it must have felt like a disaster striking a world only tangentially connected to theirs, like when one hears about an apartment fire in a distant city or an earthquake in a far-off country. On television or in grainy newsprint, one sees only the charred cinder or the toppled wall. So, part of my aim in this book is to place readers within the lived experience and the cultural context of the album's release. Even for those of us who were in the middle of it in the 1990s, it takes mental work to reconstruct that world with the emotions and events that shaped it.

Why Talk About Sex?

The frankness that characterizes the overall *Red Hot + Blue* project responds to the need to speak out about love and its ever-increasing dangers. Certainly, gestures such as wearing a red ribbon were important, but the reality of the virus demanded that people speak openly about sexual matters and that they acknowledge how love itself is a political issue. Living in The Castro, San Francisco's gay neighborhood, I felt like I saw the slogan "Silence = Death" everywhere. Whether in a shop window, across a t-shirt, or on a flier posted to a telephone pole, the phrase was often accompanied by the pink triangle, that same symbol which gay people were forced to wear in Nazi concentration camps (Figure 1.2). The presence of that triangle in two periods of persecution offers a reminder that tracing queer histories is not always empowering. Connecting these two points emphasizes that refusing to speak up can result in the eradication of those who need the supportive voices of people not like them.

We hear resonances of the same impulse to speak up in another slogan associated with AIDS activism: "Read My Lips." The simple phrase trolls President Bush by parodying his false 1998 promise, "Read my lips: no new taxes." The activist slogan is often accompanied by an image of a same-sex couple kissing.[9] The same demand to speak openly about AIDS and about same-sex desire appears in the artwork for *Red Hot + Blue*'s insert booklet. The phrase "aids is a four letter word so is love" is emblazoned across an artful photograph of a nude woman in profile.[10]

Figure 1.2 Close-up of American activist and co-founder of the Gay Teachers Association Marc Rubin (1932–2007) during an ACT UP (AIDS Coalition to Unleash Power) protest in front of St. Patrick's Cathedral, New York, New York, December 1, 1990. His t-shirt reads "Silence=Death." (Photo by Rita Barros/Getty Images).

In its earliest moments, the official response to the epidemic was one of pernicious silence. It is this legacy of silence against which *Red Hot + Blue* revolts. The necessary audacity of the album's honesty is thrown into relief if we eavesdrop briefly on an early press conference at the Reagan White House. Even as I re-read it now, I am struck by a feeling of disbelief at its disregard toward the value of gay lives. The conversation is happening between Reagan's press secretary Larry Speakes and journalist Lester Kinsolving in 1982. By this time, nearly 1,000 people have already died from AIDS in the United States:

Kinsolving:	Does the president have any reaction to the announcement by the Center for Disease Control in Atlanta that AIDS is now an epidemic in over 600 cases?
Speakes:	AIDS? I haven't got anything on it.
Kinsolving:	Over a third of them have died. It's known as "gay plague." [Press pool laughter.] No, it is. It's a pretty serious thing. One in every three people that get this have died. And I wonder if the president was aware of this.
Speakes:	I don't have it. Do you? [Press pool laughter.] Do you?
Kinsolving:	You don't have it? Well, I'm relieved to hear that, Larry! [Press pool laughter.]
Speakes:	Do you?
Kinsolving:	No, I don't.
Speakes:	You didn't answer my question. How do you know? [Press pool laughter.][11]

There's so much here in a minute or so of dialogue—the threat of a disease that kills at least one-third of those infected, the fact the White House has nothing to say, the notion that it's a "gay plague"—but really it's the laughter that gets to me. And the sad thing is, the really tragic thing is, that I'm not shocked by the laughter. What gets me is just how familiar that laughter feels. It seems like that masculine laughter at jokes about gay people—among movie audiences, during stand-up routines, from friends simply sitting around on a Saturday night—punctuating that period before I came out to people I knew. And, after that, I was left wondering if such laughter continued out of my earshot, in conversations, theaters, and clubs to which I was no longer a visitor. The press pool's collective chuckling is even more chilling when you listen to the recordings.

Kinsolving does try to put the conversation back on the rails and even seems to call out the press corps out regarding their laughter at his questions:

Kinsolving: Does the president—in other words, the White House—look on this as a great joke?

Speakes will of course say no and then (of course) will continue with the attempt at humor, as if gay (sick or dying) men are irresistible occasions for a well-deserved laugh.

Speakes: No, I don't know anything about it, Lester. There's been no personal experience here, Lester.
Kinsolving: No, I mean, I thought you were keeping …
Speakes: I don't think so. Doctor … I checked thoroughly with Dr. Ruge [the president's

> personal physician] this morning. He's
> had no … [press corps laughter]
> … no patient suffered from AIDS or
> whatever it is.

And then Kinsolving seems to give in. His courage can only stand up for so long. It seems easier to buy into the whole thing as a joke:

Kinsolving: The President doesn't have gay plague?
                   Is that what you're saying or what?
Speakes: Nope.

It isn't the immediate dismissal about the disease or the juvenile way that solely the mention of "gay" generates laughter. It's not the sense that the disease doesn't seem to matter to them. It's not that the whole thing ends up being a joke that the president might have a gay disease. The simple truth here is that no one wants to talk about or listen to other people talk about it. The reality is that they really saw gay lives as trivial or less valid than their own. AIDS couldn't affect their own lives because it was a gay disease, and so there was no reason to discuss gay people dying. And no one seems to remember that lesson from history: Silence = Death.

But it's not over. There's more. The two men can't let it go now. It's so much fun to keep baiting each other:

Speakes: I thought I heard you were in the State
                   Department over there. Why didn't you
                   stay over there?

Kinsolving:	Because I love YOU, Larry!
	[press pool laughter.]
Speakes:	Oh, I see … well, I don't … Let's don't put
	in those terms, Lester.
	[press corps laughter]
Kinsolving:	I retract that!
	[press corps laughter]
Speakes:	I hope so.

These transcripts are available to the public, but I take them from the audio recordings contained in Scott Calnico's 2015 film *When AIDS Was Funny*. The entire film might be called a horror film rather than a documentary. There's a counter showing AIDS deaths that keeps rising while successive press conferences continue to be marked by this same male banter, this same laughter from the press corps. There are jokes about "fairies," the president banning mouth-to-mouth kissing, and whether reporters have been "checked" for AIDS. It's always accompanied by guffaws from the press corps crowd. Sometimes it's hard to hear the questions and answers over the laughter from the crowd.

The funny thing—insofar as anything is funny in this scene—is that Kinsolving is a conservative radio show host. He was a fervent opponent of gay rights efforts and referred to gay rights organizations as "the sodomy lobby." Yet he's the person actually calling out the White House on their refusal to see reality. Well, he's trying and failing until he's contributing to the comedic dismissal.

Maybe it's that AIDS was too hot a topic for the White House to touch, or maybe it was pure callousness that explains how folks in the administration and the press corps thought no one would care about a disease striking down gay people. The laughter seems to imply the latter.

Too Darn Hot

The video for Erasure's version of "Too Darn Hot" on *Red Hot + Blue* opens with Andy Bell in a suit and tie. He's a television newscaster at a desk with news about the virus. We find a suburban family comfortably eating their dinner while the evening news plays on the television before them. Yet everyone in the room wears a red blindfold, highlighting the refusal by those who think HIV/AIDS does not affect them (Figure 1.3). Vince Clark is interviewing everyday people on the street, but they only want to talk about the weather. It's a deep summer swelter. Could anything be bigger news or more inconvenient than that?

Directed by Adelle Lutz and Sandy McLeod, the video juxtaposes vintage black-and-white film from the 1950s with the reality of the virus. There's a girl trying to break the local record for how many times a person can bounce on a trampoline. A housewife in an apron giddily dances while flipping hamburgers on a stove. There's a conga line, a boxing match, and a man in clowny shorts near a rotary fan just trying to stay cool. Oh, and there's a shelf full of books about how to relax. These people are focused on anything but politics, inequity, or danger. It's another take on the history of silence where people have been told what the news is, what to complain about, what a normal life looks like. The British

Figure 1.3 Erasure, "Too Darn Hot (*Red Hot + Blue*)" (Dir. Adelle Lutz and Sandy McLeod, Chrysalis Records, 1990), screenshot from the music video.

duo wants to use this Cole Porter classic to tell us that it's all crap.

These vintage scenes of hot summer days in the suburbs are undercut with newsreel style messages at the bottom of the screen. We're told that the things we see portrayed (mosquito bites, public restrooms, public phones, swimming pools, and sneezing) do not transmit the virus. The happy, go-lucky scenes of suburban white families are alternated with news reports about the widespread nature of the disease (156 countries report cases of AIDS, 8–10 million people globally are estimated to be HIV-positive, and one-third of those infected are women). As the video progresses, the archival scenes of blissful suburbia are juxtaposed by another kind of archival footage: newsreels of AIDS activists occupying the street as they protest the Centers for Disease Control and Prevention, the National Institutes of Health, and the White House. They're marching, being dragged off by police, and staging die-ins. So the blissful ignorance of untouchable normalcy collides with the message that this public rage cannot be ignored. Erasure's "Too Darn Hot" wants to show us how regimes exert their power through a refusal to recognize the people or behaviors they want to suppress. It's an exertion of "policing desire," to borrow the title of one of the great books about the epidemic by AIDS activist and educator Simon Watney (who wrote the liner notes for *Red Hot + Blue*).

The video emphasizes the damning fact that the US government is doing so little about AIDS. A screen behind our newscaster cites President Reagan's refusal to speak about the disease so that "By the time Ronald Reagan acknowledged the crisis, 25,644 people had died of AIDS." It's funny (and again I'm using the term when there isn't anything laughable about it) that Reagan only finally spoke about AIDS on the same day that Rock Hudson, Reagan's close personal friend and fellow screen icon, died from the disease.[12] That was 1985, three years after the press conference quoted above.[13]

The video ends with the roving reporter interviewing one last couple. It's an older pair. She's the housewife who was cooking so giddily earlier. He's a beat cop who earlier just wanted to talk about the weather. The husband gives the wife a peck on the cheek as they meet on the street. The traditional British couple then jointly holds up a hexagonal sign that says, "Stop," and a moment later the word "AIDS" appears on the sign. That couple has a message for us: "Stop AIDS." So we're left with hope that the message is getting through.

In exchange for letting Carlin use Porter's music, the composer's estate had wanted assurance *Red Hot + Blue*'s promotional materials would make no mention of Porter's homosexuality.[14] It's as if they wanted to maintain the blissful normalcy captured in the old-timey images in the Erasure video. Or, better yet, those idealized scenes of wholesome love from those old films starring Rock Hudson or Ronald Reagan. Yet Porter's songs demand the listener to imagine the hottest scenarios possible, even when the lyrics don't talk about sex at all. The lyrics of "Too Darn Hot" don't talk directly about sex. They just give us one of those lists that Porter loves so much and asks us to make the connection: marines, sweltering weather, a thermometer, and the Kinsey Report. It's like that other Porter hit "Let's Do It," which tells us that bees do it and birds do it. So do educated fleas, sponges, electric eels, lazy jellyfish, and so on. That song doesn't need to tell us that it's making love that all these folks are doing. I think we all know what it means to talk about the birds and the bees. It's this power of his innuendo that led Stephen Sondheim to call Porter "the dirtiest writer on Broadway."[15] All that the videos for *Red Hot and Blue* are doing is showing us what we already know: we're already thinking about sex. So, we can and should talk about it.

Notes

1. In one instance, Gladys Knight performed it with a group of adorable mummies on an episode of the Muppets. See Melissa Block, "Night And Day," *NPR.org* (June 25, 2000). Retrieved September 22, 2023.

2. Stephen Hicks, "Red Hot + 30 Years Old: How a Group of Activists Made an HIV Charity a Musical Iconoclast," *The Body* (November 25, 2019). Accessed October 1, 2023. https://www.thebody.com/article/red-hot-30-years-activists-hiv-charity-musical https://www.thebody.com/article/red-hot-30-years-activists-hiv-charity-musical

3. Stephen Holden, "Why Cole Porter Prevails—Be It Pop, Rock or Even Rap," *The New York Times* (October 21, 1990), 34H.

4. Ethan Mordden, "Critic at Large: Rock and Cole," *The New Yorker* (October 28, 1991): 110.

5. William McBrien, *Cole Porter: A Biography* (New York: Vintage Books, 2000), 249.

6. McBrien, *Cole Porter: A Biography,* 248–9.

7. McBrien, *Cole Porter: A Biography*, 248–50.

8. *Tongues Untied* Dir. Marlon Riggs 1989.

9. Both the "Silence=Death" and the "Read My Lips" graphics were designed by the Gran Fury collective. The graphics appeared in posters, wheat-pasting, guerilla painting, postcards, and small print media and, in turn, would influence a whole generation of brand advertisers and activists that came after them. The collective consisted of eleven artists and described themselves as a "band of individuals united in anger and dedicated to exploiting the power of art to end the AIDS crisis."

LET'S NOT TALK ABOUT LOVE

10. The tension between those who would speak openly about love and those who would censor free expression remains unresolved today. Consider the recent "No H8" campaign, where celebrities bore this slogan on tape across their mouths in protest of California's 2008 Proposition 8, which amended the state Constitution to ban same-sex marriage. The campaign has continued with the same taped mouth and same slogan coming to symbolize resistance to myriad forms of hate.

11. The text here is drawn from the audio recordings in *When AIDS Was Funny* (Berlin: Dir. Scott Calonico, AD&D Productions, 2015).

12. Nine weeks before his death, Hudson contacted Nancy Reagan and implored her to help him be transferred to Percy Military Hospital in France, where he could be seen by the promising specialist Dr. Dominique Dormant. Hudson's request was denied.

13. Imagine a close friend dying and not speaking up. It's as if Reagan was so invested in the fictions of normalcy that his and Hudson's films thrived upon that he could not face a reality which did not mirror Hollywood fantasy.

14. Jim Farber, "Red Hot at 30: How Compilations Used Big Music Stars to Combat AIDS," *The Guardian* (September 25, 2020). Accessed October 19, 2023. https://www.theguardian.com/music/2020/sep/25/red-hot-at-30-aids-music

15. Stephen Sondheim, *Look, I Made a Hat: Collected Lyrics (1981–2011) with Attendant Comments, Amplifications, Dogmas, Harangues, Digressions, Anecdotes and Miscellany* (New York: Knopf, 2011), 340.

2

Always True to You in My Fashion

Like the Erasure video, almost all of the songs on *Red Hot + Blue* rely on their videos to suggest how they might apply to the pandemic. Indeed, without the videos, many of the songs could just be dismissed as cover versions meant to raise money rather than vehicles for AIDS awareness messaging. But the songs on *Red Hot + Blue* can't be disaggregated from their videos as the album was really part of a conceived multimodal project. Recall that this album came out in the midst of the boom in music video production, where a song's meaning could (at last!) be derived when the video came out. So the videos themselves are part and parcel of the songs. And they're done with such vision by major artists.

But there are two songs on the album that take serious liberty with the source material as they strive to foreground AIDS awareness. The artists most influenced by hip-hop, and perhaps most deeply aware of the effect of AIDS on black communities, are the boldest in their messaging. The songs by Neneh Cherry and by The Jungle Brothers do not mince words when they confront us head-on with the dangers of AIDS.

I've Got You under My Skin

One of the most explicitly re-imagined songs is Cherry's version of "I've Got You under My Skin." It was the lead single on the album, and it rose to number 25 on the UK Singles Chart. It also achieved top-10 status in Greece and top-20 status in the Netherlands and Sweden. And it is arguably the biggest departure from what Porter aficionados might know. As one reviewer puts it, the song is

> pretty much unrecognizable from the original tinkly-suave piano nugget loved by pub singers and talent show chancers the world over [because it] starts with a rap, leads into a rubbery "White Lines" bass squiggle, before steel thwacks and programmed claps enclose the song in a glistening metal case.[1]

The reviewer is not wrong. Cherry opens the song by insisting that we join her in the reality of the pandemic rather than enter some timeless, internal world of romantic longing. In rap, she tells us that a group of people have been left in the cold, "Caught by a plague slowly they fade/From an immune deficiency, you see, called AIDS." She then relates a cautionary tale about a woman named Mary Jane, who likes to get high and, as a consequence, dies. We don't need a video to tease out the innuendo of the song or the apt implication of how having someone else under your skin might imply infection with a virus from another person, especially when one injects a shared needle under the skin. Still, the video (shot in sober blues and reds, and directed by Jean-Baptiste Mondino) makes the messaging crystal clear.

Figure 2.1 Neneh Cherry, "I've Got You under My Skin (*Red Hot + Blue*)" (Dir. Jean-Baptiste Mondino, Chrysalis Records, 1990), screenshot from the music video.

It ends with a message on screen: "Share Your Love. Don't Share the Needle" (Figure 2.1).

To talk about the dangers of sharing needles involves touching on a taboo subject. While legal needle exchange programs started much earlier in Canada and in Europe to curb the spread of hepatitis B and HIV, it was only in the mid-1980s that the first illegal programs began to operate in the United States. It took local states of emergency to circumvent laws against distributing syringes as drug paraphernalia. By 1990, both legal and illegal needle exchange programs were operating in all the large cities in the United States. Like

Cherry's video, the television special did not shy away from frank talk about the risks of transmission from injection drug use as Richard Gere states,

> Now here's the most important thing you need to know. If you have sex, wear a condom. If you're stupid enough to shoot drugs, for God's sake don't ever share the needle.

The warning means well, I'm sure, but it's hard not to hear some victim-blaming and desire-shaming around drug use that one hears elsewhere about gay desire. "All People With AIDS Are Innocent," one of the pieces of artwork in the album booklet tells us. That idea is a hard one for some people to wrap their heads around even now.

But just because Cherry's version talks about the virus directly does not mean it loses the nuance of Porter's original. Her original rap lyrics are punctuated by the refrain of the title of the song. That refrain urges us to ask, what is it that gets "under my skin" for the singer? Even though this new version centers on viral transmission, the context of a largely sexually transmitted disease leaves me meditating on love's invasive quality. Love gets under someone's hide and does not let go. But now we're also thinking about the injection of drugs. And we're considering how having unprotected sex or sharing needles can pass the virus.

Village Voice music critic Milo Miles also found compelling the direct link between Cherry's version and its overt public health messaging: "The turnabout of the title phrase in the midst of a warning about needles and AIDS," he says, is "a hook both scary and ingenious."[2] And while some reviewers found this departure to be the highlight of the album, others treated it with disdain, reflecting larger culture and genre wars with claims like "rap isn't music."[3] But we might ask: how else could Cherry have made her version? The story of Mary Jane losing her life to AIDS is one so compelling that the singer has to tell us about it, and that straight talk demands spoken word.

I Get a Kick Out of You

Like Cherry's version of a Cole Porter classic, The Jungle Brothers' "I Get a Kick Out of You" replaces most of Porter's lyrics with new ones in order to discuss directly how to prevent transmission. In this case, the song's about safer sex. Their version of the song is even more explicit than Cherry's. We're told twice about condoms, and we're taken into a scene of a cheating spouse having sex with a stranger. The song is filled with advice similar to those early HIV prevention messages. One night of lovemaking is not worth risking your life over. Kissing and body contact without penetration can be hot on their own. Sexual desire is natural. Abstinence-only strategies don't work for everyone. And, of course, always have a condom with you. As the new lyrics put it, "I wore the jimmy hat/Cause you know I'm not going out like that."

All of this advice might sound like common sense now. But, even in 1990, health educators were still working to place the focus on *harm reduction* or *risk reduction*. They'd learned that it didn't work to completely deny the sway of desire or to tell people to stop acting on their desires. Instead, what made sense was to help people understand how to do what they wanted to do but to do it more safely.

Originally, Lou Reed was in the queue to record "I Get a Kick Out of You," and the video would have been directed by Martin Scorsese. Ultimately, the track was recorded by The Jungle Brothers with Mark Pellington directing the video. The television networks might have preferred Reed doing the version. Carlin has described racist reactions toward the idea of a hip hop group in the television special (connecting to the "rap isn't music" comment by one reviewer speaking about Cherry's song). "They kept calling them The Jungle Bunnies," Carlin recalls. "Maybe once is a slip. But after that, you've just revealed your feelings."[4] As risqué as this new version may sound, it's interesting to note that Porter's original was risqué in its day. The lyrics mention cocaine and drinking, even if they do so to say that these indulgences are inferior to love. Both versions ultimately contemplate how our desires exist on a spectrum, and we might as well admit that people have their vices. The key is to prioritize how and with whom you indulge in them.

How Could We Be Wrong?

The presence of these two songs overtly discussing AIDS (while the other tracks did not) left some reviewers wrestling with the thematic cohesion of the album. The album is a mix, to be sure. Certainly, its songs in their original forms don't directly talk about disease and perhaps only obliquely talk about homosexuality. They're not the most obvious choice for an album doing HIV awareness and prevention work.

Consider how David Browne, writing in *Entertainment Weekly,* finds himself trying to make sense of the choice of Cole Porter songs:

> The choice of Porter's giddy, jaunty '30s and '40s love songs is itself meant as a comment on the safe-sex era. We're supposed to listen to these versions and feel nostalgic for—and angry about—the demise of the romantic era in which Porter lived and wrote.

But I don't really think that's it. First, of course, there would be a range of reactions to the songs. But I believe it would be counter-productive if the album aimed to leave listeners blaming the virus (or those who spread it) for ruining the traditional mystique of love. The album helps us make sense of what was happening in the pandemic because of Porter's timelessness.[5] Carlin explains that he chose Porter not because of the perfect romantic world the composer inhabited but rather because of his vexed relationship to that ideal:

> Cole Porter was the original creative spark—songs by a closeted gay man that your grandmother loved—that became the perfect foundation for both the first successful tribute album and one dedicated to AIDS awareness and LGBTQ rights.[6]

Browne and Carlin might seem to be making opposite claims about the album's relationship to history. But I think they're both right, in the sense that they (in different ways) perceive the album as an engine for nostalgia.

Carlin seems to understand that Porter's music can be many things at once. It can be profoundly romantic and sentimental. But it can also undermine the sincerity of these feelings. Part of what seems to pester Browne is the variety of tones on the album:

> But picking a cause is one thing; deciding whether these songs should be treated as camp classics or masterworks of pop craft is another. Despite its good intentions, *Red Hot & Blue* doesn't address that problem.[7]

This variety, like the album's complex relationship to nostalgia, is something that I address in a subsequent chapter. Let me briefly say here, though, that I think Porter himself developed songs that were frivolous camp and songs that were more carefully crafted pop tunes, and that I'm not sure we can always disaggregate one form from the other. It's important to remember that Porter wrote over 800 songs in his lifetime, many of which defy strict categorization.

Allow me to spend a moment more on Browne's review which, toward its end, hits on a really crucial issue about how to interpret the purpose of *Red Hot + Blue*. Part of his contention involves how this album is supposed to function in relation to the AIDS crisis. He does not mention The Jungle Brothers' "I Get a Kick Out of You." Instead, he centers on "I've Got You under My Skin" and "From This Moment On" as the two explicit interventions on the album:

> Throughout all of this, we're too distracted for any point to be conveyed. Aside from Cherry's rap, the personal impact of the AIDS crisis emerges only on "From This

Moment On," with its creamy, desperate wail by Jimmy Somerville, former lead singer of Bronski Beat and one of pop's few openly gay artists. When Somerville wraps his siren-like voice around Porter's sorrowful lyrics, we feel both the allure of romance and its loss; the song becomes universal and moving.[8]

This assessment misses, among other things, the personal connection the other artists (including David Byrne) might have to the epidemic or the presence of other openly gay artists (Andy Bell) among the contributors. To assume that the "personal impact" of the album emerges only from Somerville's version reinforces one of the assumptions about the disease that the album sought to address: that it was only a concern of gay men. I think this misses the diversity of people described as affected by AIDS (the straight adulterer in The Jungle Brothers' lyrics, the global population of women highlighted in Erasure's video). It also misses the foundation of allyship upon which the whole album is rooted.

I invoke this particular review at length not really to criticize Browne but instead to tease out the challenges to be overcome in fully comprehending this album (and perhaps any tribute album) and its relationship to members of communities disproportionately affected by AIDS (but really any individuals for whom love and desire are vexed topics). Certainly, other critics felt *Red Hot + Blue* was not as directly linked to the epidemic as it could be. A reviewer in Boston's *Gay Community News* felt the album ranked as "easily the best multi-artist collection yet and includes what has to be some of the finest work by some of the artists."[9] However, it was "great work that could be greater only by being gayer, or more AIDS-related."[10]

I'm mostly struck by the shared tension across these reviews around the question of whether Porter can speak to a new era. I feel the answer to that question has already been provided by the versatility of his work across musical history. Even during his lifetime, he did not hold his lyrics as sacrosanct. "I Get a Kick Out of You," for example, originally had a reference to Anne Spencer Morrow Lindbergh. And Porter omitted this in a revision done after the kidnapping of the Lindbergh baby in 1932. Then he altered the song again to align with the Hollywood Production Code, sometimes called the "Hays Code," which outlined moral guidelines for what should be included in films. Porter changed the song's opening reference to people who "get a kick from cocaine" to those who "like the perfume in Spain" for the 1936 film version of the musical *Anything Goes,* where "I Get a Kick Out of You" was sung by Ethel Merman.

And, since his death, Porter's music has been adapted by so many artists. It would be difficult to overestimate Porter's influence on music history and English-speaking culture writ large. Alongside Irving Berlin, George Gershwin, Jerome Kern, and Richard Rodgers, he generated the foundation to the American Songbook. I think this says something not only about the inherent changeability of his work but also about the legitimizing effect of his music. And it's the combination of these two things that makes his music the ideal choice for *Red Hot + Blue*. Covers of his songs have allowed some of the best-known voices in American music to enter the mainstream or place themselves in the genealogy of musical history. Artists such as not only Ella Fitzgerald but also Rosemary Clooney, Harry Connick, Jr., and Frank Sinatra might be good examples of this.[11] Or some artists might seek to justify their claims to cross-genre or cross-generation appeal. Consider tribute albums by artists such as Dionne Warwick, Harry Connick Jr., and Ella Fitzgerald. Or consider an album such as Tony Bennett's and Lady Gaga's 2021 joint effort *Love for Sale*. This one represents a kind of merging of different traditions as well as different generations. Because Porter's work and his influence are so pervasive, it would be difficult to identify a single album or Broadway soundtrack to capture it. Porter left an indelible mark on American music and has been inducted into the American Theater Hall of Fame, Great American Songbook Hall of Fame, and the Hollywood Walk of Fame.[12]

The choice of Cole Porter's music was an evocative one. In some ways, he exemplified the lighthearted, untouchable society whose foundations *Red Hot + Blue* sought to shake. In other ways, however, Porter's own life story was one marked by the themes of prejudice and loss that the artists sought to illuminate. As we will see in the chapters that follow, the album strives to chronicle a universal experience while also pinpointing elements of the epidemic that many people did not want to talk about but that needed to be talked about.

From This Moment On

While I do not agree with Browne's overall assessment of the album, I do hear what he's saying about Jimmy Somerville as the ideal choice for the album. Who better, really, to bring to life Porter's paeans of private longing and exuberant desire? The singer's distinctive sound on that Bronski Beat 1984 hit "Smalltown Boy" is one of the definitive voices of queer heartache during the decade preceding *Red Hot + Blue*. The song appears on the album *Age of Consent* (which features the pink triangle on its cover). "Smalltown Boy," as well as Somerville's 1989 cover of "You Make Me Feel (Mighty Real)" on the solo album *Read My Lips*, was in regular rotation at the tea dance I would go to Sunday afternoons at the I-Beam club in San Francisco. That latter song was originally recorded by Sylvester, the disco singer who shared Somerville's love of falsetto and who died from AIDS-related complications in 1988. What I remember from the I-Beam are those and other pop or disco-inspired songs. And I remember pamphlets about HIV transmission. And my friend Ray saying that you could tell who had it and who didn't.

Unlike the Erasure video for "Too Darn Hot," Somerville's video (directed by Steve McLean) for "From This Moment On" is all about private intimacy. Erasure had a roving reporter on the streets, a five-alarm newscast, and a sea of activists in front of the White House. Somerville serenades two shirtless men embracing. Yet I see both videos as capturing essential elements of AIDS activism. The two representations, in very different ways, bring private feeling to the public front. The protesters are demanding that same-sex love be recognized as equally valid as heterosexual love and that queer bodies be seen as equally worth protecting. Isn't that what Somerville is also asking for with close-ups on the intertwined torsos of two men in love?

Thinking about the shared investments of both scenes—the crowd of protesters and the private lovers—I am reminded of the call-to-action, "An Army of Lovers Cannot Lose." The AIDS activist groups ACT UP and Queer Nation used the phrase in a pamphlet at the June 1990 New York Gay Pride Parade. It's an idea with a long history, and it's an idea that shows us the far reach of gay history. The phrase echoes a famous claim from Plato's *Symposium*, in which it is said that an "army of lovers" could "though few, conquer all." This seems to be a reference to the so-called Sacred Band of Thebes, an elite force of 150 pairs of male lovers fighting in the Theban army. Their private love shared within pairs motivates them to protect each other, as Plutarch tells us, and their public, shared love of their community motivates them to fight as a single entity. It's a wonderful analogy for political activism fighting for the right to love, and it also speaks aptly for a tribute album where artists come together to sing songs of love.

Notes

1. Paul Lester, "Singles," *Melody Maker* (September 22, 1990): 35.

2. Milo Miles, "Cole Cuts: Cole Porter, Fresh for 1990," *Village Voice* (November 20, 1990): 85.

3. Mordden, "Rock and Cole," *New Yorker* (October 28, 1991): 110.

4. Jim Farber, "Red Hot at 30: How Compilations Used Big Music Stars to Combat AIDS," *The Guardian* (September 25, 2020). Accessed October 19, 2023. https://www.theguardian.com/music/2020/sep/25/red-hot-at-30-aids-music

5.   *Red Hot + Blue* was one of several projects that
     commemorated the 100th anniversary of Porter's birth
     and "serves as a reminder of the timeless quality of Porter's
     songcraft," as Mark Heim remarked in his review in *The
     Chicago Tribune*. Chris Heim, "*Red Hot + Blue* Benefit Album
     Shines," *Chicago Tribune* (December 14, 1990): O.

6.   Neal Broverman, "Revisiting *Red Hot + Blue*, the Most Iconic
     HIV Charity Album Ever," *Plus Magazine* (December 1, 2020).
     Retrieved October 28, 2023. https://www.hivplusmag.com/
     print-issue/2020/12/01/revisiting-red-hot-blue-most-iconic-
     hiv-benefit-album-ever

7.   David Browne, "Red Hot & Blue," *Entertainment Weekly*
     (2, 1990). Accessed August 15, 2023. https://ew.com/
     article/1990/11/02/red-hot-blue-2/

8.   Browne, "Red Hot & Blue."

9.   Walta Borawski, "Too, Too Hot: The New Collection of Cole
     Porter Songs, *Red Hot & Blue,* Recorded to Benefit AIDS
     Research and Relief, Could Only Be Better by Being Gayer,
     or More AIDS-Related," *Gay Community News* Boston 18.18
     (November 17, 1990): 20.

10. The reviewer does praise the materials and packaging: "On the
     positive side, the word 'AIDS' does appear on the cover art,
     and little booklets accompanying the cassette and compact
     disc have [...] AIDS information. And one of the booklets
     includes a lovely landscape with the words: 'all people with
     aids are innocent' superimposed over it." Borawski, "Too,
     Too Hot."

11. Norman Granz, Fitzgerald's manager, urged her specifically to
     record an album of Cole Porter songs because it could connect
     her with a broad, popular market. He recalls, "I was interested
     in how I could enhance Ella's position, to make her a singer

with more than just a cult following amongst jazz fans. [...]
So I proposed to Ella that the first Verve album would not
be a jazz project, but rather a song book of the works of Cole
Porter." Qtd. in Ted Hershorn, *Norman Granz: The Man Who
Used Jazz for Justice* (Berkeley: University of California Press,
2011), 217.

12. Beyond the ways in which later artists have recorded Porter's
music, there is also the legacy of the songs he influenced. It
would take a whole book to name all of these. So, I'll just echo
Carlin's point in the liner notes: "a direct parallel can be drawn
between the simple power of Porter's 'Let's Do It, Let's Fall
in Love' and John Lennon's 'All You Need Is Love' or, for that
matter, between Porter's 'Let's Misbehave' and Prince's 'Let's
Go Crazy.'" John Carlin, liner notes, *Red Hot + Blue* (Chrysalis
Records, 1990).

3

Another Opinion, Another Show

The coupling of two shirtless men in Somerville's video was just one of several instances of tension around the airing of *Red Hot + Blue*'s television special. The commissioning editor of Britain's Channel Four complained that the sight of an inter-racial, same-sex couple embracing without shirts was "a little too specific" because it invoked "a touch of the 'Shock-Horror' syndrome."[1] We hear so clearly in this comment how the editor simultaneously prioritizes a viewer who might be uncomfortable with the idea of same-sex love and suggests that the bodies of such lovers are somehow less normal than others. The producers of the American version wanted to cut sections of Sinéad O'Connor video because it featured two women dancing (the producers did not seem to notice the two men dancing).[2] "They said, 'it's advocating lesbianism,'" John Carlin recalls. "I said, 'What's wrong with that?'"[3] When ABC produced the special in the United States, the network chose to omit Somerville's video as well as the one for Cherry's "I've Got You under My Skin."

The debate about what to include in the television special brings us back to that curious tension between Porter's canonical legacy and the charged reality of the AIDS epidemic. Carlin recalls, "We produced the show in the U.K., and it came to the United States, and the network really wanted it to be a Cole Porter special, celebrating his music and really downplay the activism."[4] It was only at the last minute that some of the most vital information about the virus was included:

> ABC wanted [Richard Gere] to read something about Cole Porter, and he asked me if I thought that was appropriate and I said no. You have to read something about the AIDS pandemic. This is why we're all here. And he said, well, what should I say? I actually wrote that script that you just played, you know, in the studio, in the green room, while he was waiting to go on and be filmed. And ABC wanted to stop him saying it, and he threatened to walk off the set if they didn't let him read it.[5]

Protest and political activism don't only happen in marches in front of government buildings. Carlin and Gere engaged in it right there, in that moment when they prioritized speaking up over fear.

The American version of the special is marked by this tug-of-war of moods. This desire to speak grates against the allure of silencing overt discussion of the epidemic. While Neneh Cherry's song opened the album, the first song featured in the special was David Byrne's "Don't Fence Me In." It's a song that's peppy, happy, and meant to be inclusive. Faces morph into each other, mouthing the words to the song as we hear Byrne's voice. The visual aesthetic predicts the face-morphing effect in the video for Michael Jackson's "Black or White" a year later. The video was originally supposed to be directed by Pedro Almodóvar, but at the last minute he was unavailable, so Byrne directed it himself. If we think hard about it, we can imagine the song as an analogue for the need to consider all kinds of people when we contemplate who might be affected by AIDS. And that universalizing impulse was indeed important to the success of the project. Carlin recalls, "It struck me that the Cole Porter songs were a wonderful way to make a contemporary record that would appeal to all sorts of people and deliver a message."[6] But the joyful tone of the song and the happy people, while making for a delightful video, works against the sense of urgency that I associate with HIV/AIDS in 1990.

Were people surprised that the television special was edited in the United States? Boraski's review of the album in *The Gay Community News* saw this coming and lamented it as the further silencing expected for the project:

By the by, British gay writer Simon Watney, who worked on this wondrous project and wrote the collection's liner notes, says that by the time the accompanying videos hit ABC on a Dec. 1 World AIDS Day special, we will be very disappointed by the de-gayifying and de-AIDS-ifying already going on as the project crosses the Atlantic Ocean. He expects the defiantly gay Somerville and Erasure videos, as well as the footage of the same sex couples dancing behind Sinéad O'Connor, to hit the cutting room floor. He also doesn't think k.d. lang's video for "So in Love" will survive the trip. In it, lang visits her woman lover in a hospital, then goes home and does their laundry, ending with a long shot of lang taking a good sniff from a pair of panties. Did you evah?[7]

It turns out that Boraski and Watney were right to be concerned. The American version was de-toothed. Malcolm Leo, the ABC producer assigned to the program, remarked: "I would definitely say this is an entertainment special designed to celebrate Cole Porter through musicians of today," going on to say, "The problem was finding the right balance so that the show wasn't a polemic."[8] So the television special itself is the result of conflicting opinions about what one can say and what one can show. A review of both versions in the *Los Angeles Times* gives us one way to think of the difference: "The British program is essentially a testament to the urgency of the AIDS crisis, supported by Porter music," while "the U.S. program is essentially a testament to Porter, with AIDS in the background."[9]

This is not to say that the US television special, which aired on World AIDS Day, December 1, 1990, was not ground-breaking. It just could have been more so. Certainly the name recognition of the directors working on the videos— Jonathan Demme, Jim Jarmusch, Jean-Baptiste Mondino, and Wim Wenders—validated the seriousness of the project. The artwork for the album and the television special also featured major names: Sue Coe, Jean-Paul Gaultier, Jenny Holzer, Gran Fury, Keith Haring, Barbara Kruger, and David Wojnarowicz. The televised show was seen globally in over thirty countries, and it spoke openly (if briefly) about a disease associated with things people weren't talking about: same-sex desire, commercial sex work, injection drug use, and the disparities in healthcare for communities of color. In fact, the show included one of the first mentions of "condom" on network US television (outside of news programming).[10]

When a Body's in Love

While the Red Hot Organization was unable to deliver those embracing toros in the ABC television special, it was able to bring much-needed frankness with its "Safe Sex Is Hot Sex" message. The print campaign aimed at increasing public awareness and involved street posters with diverse couples, gay and straight, female and male, multiple races and multiple languages (Figure 3.1).

The couples for "Safe Sex Is Hot Sex" were photographed by Steven Klein, Steven Meisel, and Bruce Weber. The posters were wheatpasted everywhere in urban centers, and I remember seeing them in San Francisco. They contributed to the effort to encourage people not to see AIDS prevention as an "all-or-nothing" equation. Instead, people could choose how much risk they felt comfortable with and could re-think what they considered to be the most erotic of activities. The posters also did important work of combatting some of the early mis-depictions of the disease as largely striking white gay men. Just as Covid has in our current era, AIDS became a flashpoint for the intersectional nature of public health and social justice. "Safe Sex Is Hot Sex" demanded that people see this as a disease striking all types of bodies and affirmed

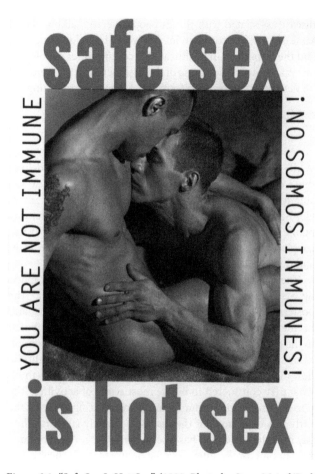

Figure 3.1 "Safe Sex Is Hot Sex" (1990, Photo by Steve Meisel/Red Hot Organization).

that those bodies deserved equal access to health care and to sexual expression.

The sad truth was that such campaigns needed community-based fundraising because of the government's refusal to speak openly and equally about sexuality. In 1987, Congress passed an amendment specifically denying federal funding to any educational materials that mentioned same-sex relations or injection drug use in a positive light. The amendment prohibited "the use of any funds" to

> provide AIDS education, information, or prevention materials and activities that promote, encourage, and condone homosexual sexual activities or the intravenous use of illegal drugs.[11]

Senator Jesse Helms was one of the major proponents of the legislation, and it was signed into law by President Reagan.[12]

But such prudery was not just the purview of the United States, and this kind of silence was not just about AIDS education. During the same period, Britain was cast under the shadow of "Section 28," legislation that involved several laws which prohibited the "promotion of homosexuality" by local authorities. It was in effect from 1988 to 2000 in Scotland and from 1988 to 2003 in England and Wales.[13] The law is named after Section 28 of the Local Government Act 1988, which added Section 2A to the Local Government Act 1986. The amendment asserted that a local authority shall not "intentionally promote homosexuality or publish material with the intention of promoting homosexuality" nor may it "promote the teaching in any maintained school of the acceptability of homosexuality as a pretended family relationship."[14]

And have we really come far from those dark days? What's past is prologue, as Shakespeare once remarked. The legislation circulating in the time of *Red Hot + Blue* foreshadows Florida's HB 1557, also known as the "Don't Say Gay" bill, which states that "classroom instruction by school personnel or third parties on sexual orientation or gender identity may not occur in kindergarten through grade 3."[15] The American Civil Liberties Union (ACLU) is currently tracking 505 anti-LGBTQ laws in the United States. These include efforts to prohibit transgender people from using public bathrooms; to force teachers to out students; to ban drag shows; to allow employers, businesses, and even hospitals to turn away LGBTQ people or refuse them equal treatment; and to censor any in-school discussions of LGBTQ people and issues.[16]

It may feel like a cliché now to invoke that phrase from Oscar Wilde's trial, "the love that dare not speak its name," yet it strikes me that there is yet a political movement to not mention same-sex desire. And, even in writing this book, I find myself carefully choosing language to speak with a realness but perhaps, at times, not too much frankness. Maybe part of me is still that 25-year-old who felt embarrassed when his mom heard the Gay Men's Chorus put special emphasis on the words "blow," "daddy," and "top" in Porter's songs. The extensive legislation since *Red Hot & Blue*'s release, not to mention the rise in the banning of books, emphasizes that we're still worried about open discussions of sexuality. They might induce what the Channel 4 editor worried was the shock of seeing or even imagining the coupling of same-sex bodies in Jimmy Somerville's music video.

Remember that *Red Hot + Blue* came out just two years after President Clinton announced the "Don't Ask, Don't Tell" policy in 1988. So it might seem like silence was the rule around sexuality. But, for me, the period is also marked by what was said aloud and the degree to which certain kinds of speech were permitted. Why do I still recall so vividly the image of Sebastian Bach wearing a t-shirt that says "AIDS Kills Fags Dead" after a Skid Row concert in 1989? It's a revised tagline from the insecticide Raid, "Raid Kills Bugs Dead." Kurt Loder, that omnipresent MTV video jockey of my youth, did openly criticize Bach for the shirt. The Skid Row frontman did offer some contrition, though he remarked to *MTV*: "But let me just state this—I do not know, condone, comprehend, or understand homosexuality in any way, shape, form or [*laughs*] size."[17] And before we dismiss this as juvenile heavy metal culture, let's take a moment to recall that laughter brought forth from similar banter by Reagan's White House press secretary.[18]

There's so much of this type of humor in my recollection of that period when the album was released and when I was wondering if it was safe to come out as a gay person. I don't need a web search to call such hurtful phrases up from a surprisingly ready memory: "AIDS Cures Homosexuality," "AIDS = Anally Injected Death Sentence," "GAY = Got AIDS Yet?" Maybe I remember these so clearly because I was worried that these were the phrases that would come to the minds of people in high school if they learned of my sexuality. Or maybe I remember them so clearly because they have an earworm quality. In all their perniciousness, they're clever in the way that Porter's song lyrics are clever.

These aren't just jokes in extremely poor taste. They are part of a pattern of thought that associates homosexuality and disease in a way that those seeking equal rights had worked to disarm in the 1970s. In fact, AIDS arrived at a point in time when things seemed to be moving in a positive direction for gay people in the United States. Homosexuality had long been classified as a mental disorder in the *Diagnostic and Statistical Manual of Mental Disorders* (*DSM*) published by the American Psychiatric Association (APA) until gay rights activists worked together after the 1969 Stonewall riots to have it changed. In late 1973, the APA board of trustees decided to declassify homosexuality as a mental disorder in the subsequent edition of the *DSM*.[19]

But these jokes are echoes of a long-held belief that homosexuality, like HIV, functions like a virus. If you look at the early news reports about AIDS, it wasn't called AIDS. The early cases of Kaposi sarcoma were widely referred to as a mysterious "gay cancer." As more information emerged about gay men getting sick, the disease was called "Gay Related Immune Deficiency" (GRID).[20] The very fact of being gay was making people sick. It's not a big logical jump when you consider how long homosexuality was considered a disease, even one that could be transmitted. Gayness could be caught through exposure to images of same-sex desire or through exposure to gay people (hence, cultural fears that even the presence of gay people in classrooms might lead to "grooming"). Isn't this the implication of the gay panic defense in the case of the 1998 murder of Matthew Shepherd?

It's a matter of life and death if a gay person is attracted to you, and a gay person's life isn't worth as much as yours.

"I've Got You under My Skin," indeed.

Notes

1. Qtd. in Simon Watney, *Practices of Freedom: Selected Writing on HIV/AIDS* (Durham: Duke University Press, 1994), 215.

2. The producers, however, loved the video with k.d. lang. In that video, her deceased partner is clearly a woman (based on the women's clothes being washed). The absent same-sex partner, though powerfully present in the singer's mind, is less problematic than the present same-sex dance partner. John Carlin, interview by John S. Garrison, October 2, 2023.

3. Jim Farber, "Red Hot at 30: How Compilations Used Big Music Stars to Combat AIDS," *The Guardian* (September 25, 2020). Accessed October 19, 2023. https://www.theguardian.com/music/2020/sep/25/red-hot-at-30-aids-music

4. "World AIDS Day: 30 Years of Musical Activism," cnn.com (December 1, 2020). http://edition.cnn.com/transcripts/2012/01/ampr.01.html

5. "World AIDS Day: 30 Years of Musical Activism."

6. Qtd. in David Bauder, "Cole Porter Recruited for AIDS Battle Songs," *Toronto Star* (November 7, 1990).

7. Simon Watney is the author of one of the classic early texts on issues of silence in relation to the epidemic, *Policing Desire: Pornography, AIDS, and the Media* (1997). He served as Health Education Advisor for *Red Hot + Blue*. Borawski, "Too, Too Hot."

8. Qtd. in Howard Rosenberg, "ABC Takes Strides with 'Red Hot'–and Bold–Special," *Los Angeles Times* (November 30, 1990). Retrieved October 28, 2023. https://www.latimes.com/archives/la-xpm-1990-11-30-ca-5597-story.html

9. Rosenberg, "ABC Takes Strides."

10. Although I have not seen it quantified, surely one of the benefits of the special was an increase in the number of people getting an HIV test. When Magic Johnson revealed he was HIV-positive, calls to testing centers skyrocketed to twice, even six times, the normal interest level. A similar effect was caused by the premiere of *It's a Sin*—Russell T. Davis's series that depicts the first ten years of the AIDS epidemic in the UK. A startling 8,200 testing kits were ordered from The Terrence Higgins Trust in one day, more than three times the record for a single day of orders previously. Minnie Stephenson, "HIV Testing Rises as *It's a Sin* Becomes C4's Most-Watched Drama," *Channel 4 News* (February 5, 2021). Retrieved February 6, 2021; Will Richards, "Olly Alexander Says He's 'Moved' to See Record HIV Tests Following *It's a Sin*," *NME* (February 5, 2021) Retrieved February 6, 2021.

11. Jesse Helms, (October 14, 1987), "S. Amdt. 963 to H.R.3058–100th Congress (1987–1988)." *www.congress.gov*.

12. In 1993, when President Clinton presented Roberta Achtenberg as his nominee for Assistant Secretary of the Department of Housing and Urban Development, Helms attempted to stir Republican resistance by showing lawmakers a video of a kiss between Achtenberg and her partner during a gay pride parade. "Call it gay-bashing if you want to," he said. "I call it standing up for America's traditional family values." Kissing may not kill, but it still promised to irk.

13. "When Gay Became a Four-Letter Word." BBC. 20 (January 2000). Retrieved January 4, 2010.

14. "When Gay Became a Four-Letter Word."

15. "/Session/Bill/2022/1557" www.flsenate.gov

16. "Mapping Attacks on LGBTQ Rights in U.S. State Legislatures." https://www.aclu.org/legislative-attacks-on-lgbtq-rights

17. The response here is quoted in Patrick Goldstein, "Skid Row's Sebastian Bach Embroiled in AIDS Row," *Los Angeles Times* (January 21, 1990). Accessed October 28, 2023. https://www.latimes.com/archives/la-xpm-1990-01-21-ca-727-story.html

18. The incident made *Spin Magazine's* list of the fifty worst moments of the 1990s. See "Soy Un Perdedor: The 50 Worst Moments of the '90s," *Spin Magazine* (August 15, 2013). Accessed October 28, 2023. https://www.spin.com/2013/08/the-worst-moments-of-the-90s-worst-band-names-worst-lyrics-worst-video/

19. Progress is not particularly linear, and the United States is not necessarily behind the rest of the world. It was also in 1990 that the World Health Organization replaced its categorization of homosexuality as a mental illness with the diagnosis of "ego-dystonic sexual orientation" (the very condition which had been eliminated from the *DSM*).

20. For a concise and incisive snapshot of the epidemic, including how homophobia and racism informed how it was initially understood, see Schulman, *Let the Record Show,* 8–10.

4

It's Just like the Good Old Days

For all the overtness that Neneh Cherry and The Jungle Brothers bring to their re-imagined versions of the songs and for all the frankness of the prevention campaign and even the television special, *Red Hot + Blue* at heart is a series of homages to classic love songs. The tracks on the album are, after all, *standards*. Yet despite the connotations of straightforwardness inherent in that term, the songs have embedded within them intriguing complexities. Certainly, these jazz chestnuts possess a *timeless* quality as they have been recorded by so many artists during the last century. Yet in their own way, these standards are also *timely*, as they reflect the building of the American songbook which Cole Porter helped conceive as he captured the zeitgeist of a cultural moment between the world wars and translated it into song. As Johnny Mercer, the American lyricist and co-founder of Capitol Records, once put it,

> Cole Porter is definitive of an era. He is those years, you know? He is the style of all those shows, all that period.

He represents it better than anybody else, better even than Kern or Berlin. Porter's so … thirties![1]

Which is it then? Is Cole Porter's music so universal that it transcends history, or is it so powerful because it pinpoints a distinct moment in history? Certainly, it was this question that led some reviewers to see a mismatch in the choice of Porter as the object of tribute for an album about the AIDS epidemic.

The complexity of Cole Porter's standards and what they mean for us today is what makes the evening with the San Francisco Gay Men's Chorus stand out so much for me. The performance revealed his peculiar relationship to contemporary gay identity and to the AIDS crisis. During that evening and on the album, Porter's songs speak powerfully to both themes, even if his experience of being gay was quite different from the one people have now and even though he died before the AIDS epidemic occurred. Even in a world separate from the one in which Porter composed his work, his songs and his life reveal a new kind of sense to us. Perhaps that is because, as the *New York Times* review of the album put it, "Porter was a rigid pop traditionalist. But he was also an unblinking realist about life, love, pleasure, and the transience of it all."[2]

After You, Who?

One of the contributions to the album that both sounds very Porter and looks very much like the world he inhabited is Jody

Watley's "After You, Who?" It's pure torch song, especially in the video (directed by Matthew Rolston) where Watley is on stage in a supper-club wearing a diamond-studded cocktail dress. She's occasionally flirting with audience members, but mostly she seems lost in the music. And the crowd seems that way too, as if the performer is just a conduit through which listeners are transported to another time and place. Or maybe they're taken to no particular time and place at all. The music lifts them out of their current situation and into a shared zone of pure emotion. Love songs do that, don't they? They allow us to tap into, even if only for a few minutes, our own deepest romantic feeling. And not only that: they can just as effectively console us during times of heartbreak with their promise that the possibility of love is still out there.

But the video invokes that otherworldly state only to slowly erode it. We realize that Watley and her musicians are the only black people in the room. The audience is entirely white, and Watley's lover has been forced to wait outside the club. He tries to come in and listen to her, but the host won't let him in. So for the whole performance we're seeing images of him in her mind, but she can only see him in person when she exits into an alley behind the club. It's him that she's been singing about, but to have him in the club would break the spell for the audience, which needs to see the classic supper-club chanteuse as just a vehicle for the song. The singer may use the pronouns "I" and "you" when singing, but her personal feelings are not truly at stake for the club audience. Rather, she offers herself as the means by which listeners can imagine themselves saying the lyrics or having those lyrics said to them.

So for all the ways that the lyrics of "After You, Who?" celebrate union with the ideal lover, the video underscores issues of separation. Reflecting on her decision to participate in *Red Hot + Blue,* Watley recalls that "My label didn't want me to do it because they thought my participation would give the impression that I was either gay or had the virus."[3] The label's concerns show how the AIDS crisis revealed how homophobia and stigma around the disease were genuine threats to public health because they deterred people from speaking up. The video emphasizes that the social discrimination about whom one can love and what kind of love should be shown in public was already embedded in Porter's era. There have always been people who are not part of the mainstream—because of how they look, what they believe, who they desire, and whether they are perceived to be sick—and this has always been policed.

We see this vividly in the video. The all-white audience and the excluded lover showcase how on-screen or on-stage depictions often obscure just how diverse forms of love can be. The scenario of racial segregation in the music video offers the perfect analogue for the way that Porter's gay experience might be sublimated into his music. Yet the audience doesn't want to see the man who Watley's character might be singing to, just as the Porter estate didn't want any explicit mention of the composer's homosexuality in *Red Hot + Blue*'s materials.[4] And this speaks to how silence about diverse forms of love slowed responses to the AIDS epidemic.

Nostalgia, I think, has a curious relationship to the interleaved histories of love and sex. It wouldn't be the whole story to say that the songs on this album invoke a nostalgia for a period before AIDS. It's true that they invoke a time when having sex did not have so close an association with a sexually transmitted infection that was life-threatening. But having sex has always carried risks of some sort, whether emotional or physical. The music derives from a period when sex and love were dangerous for those who lacked power or were marked as different from the perceived majority, in a culture that would suppress news of domestic abuse as well as disavow same-sex and cross-race relationships. It is still surprising to me that *Loving v. Virginia* only reached the supreme court in 1967, when eighteen states still enforced laws against marriages between white people and people of color. So it's not that Porter's music depicts a simpler time or a more traditional view of love. But it is true that his songs sometimes strip the intricacies of love down to the emotion's pure form, and the idea that we might experience love without complication might have been a kind of wish-fulfillment for Porter.

Love songs, for all their explicit claims to express the singular love between two people, thrive on ambiguity. And that ambiguity is especially present in these standards from the jazz age. It's why they work. "The popular market," to which Porter's lyrics contribute, where the songs are sung by many artists over time, involve "androgynous lyrics—a genderless 'I' cooing to an equally indeterminate 'you' that could be performed by either male or female vocalists, insuring their widest commercial dissemination."[5] It's this indeterminacy that lets us hear a song and imagine it's describing how *we* feel. But rather than leading people to see love as a universal phenomenon between many kinds of people, the ambiguity of the genders indicated by a song's pronouns can have the opposite effect. Some fans of "From This Moment On" don't want to imagine it's a song about two men when Jimmy Somerville sings it. And they might not want to know who or what Porter was thinking about when he wrote "Let's Do It." The idea that the songs might be for everybody did not mesh with the seemingly personal nature of the lyrics. To ignore the idea that these songs might refer to same-sex couples also ignores their long history. Porter's songs experienced special popularity within gay subcultures of the 1920s and 1930s.[6]

The title of the song chosen by Watley, "After You, Who?," also helps us think about that other theme so central to the experience of AIDS: loss. The song is about "the one," or the belief that the perfect partner is out there for us. The underside of that belief, though, is the fear that there might never be someone to replace "the one" if we lose them. Of course, we know it's not true. People—well, many people—do indeed find love again after a relationship ends. But that does not mean that they forget the previous lover. That person is still a part of them, if not through ongoing attachment then in the way that the previous lover has changed the person. Indeed, we might think about the title of this song as capturing that double-action. After you, who would I possibly be with? After you, who have I become? And, while "After You, Who?" is certainly a love song, we also realize that people can transform us regardless of whether they might have been a lover, a friend, a family member, or even someone for whom we feel enmity.

"After You, Who?" sweeps us into the notion that the past spoils us for the future. It's a paradox, isn't it? We might believe that a singular love ruins us for all subsequent ones. But that idea increases the precarity of love and the readiness for its loss. Watley remarks that the songs on *Red Hot + Blue* are "poetic reminders of the importance of love, romance, empathy and desire, in an era when people were afraid to even touch one another."[7] Understood this way, each of the tracks on the album not only signals the power of love over hate but also offers the space of the song as a space of respite. And songs can be spaces of survival, whether they allow the character in the video to fantasize about an impossible union in an era of segregated spaces (which certainly persist today) or allow Porter to quietly celebrate same-sex relationships even when they were relegated to some shadow world (which they are sometimes today, too).

You Do Something to Me

Recall that Sinéad O'Connor's video for "You Do Something to Me" was one of the ones that contributed to the stir around the US broadcast of the television special. What strikes me as radical about the video, though, is not its brief inclusion of same-sex partners dancing. Rather, I'm struck by how it plays with nostalgia in a way that takes the dynamic of Watley's rendition to an even further extreme. O'Connor invokes a classic swing rhythm in her rendition, and the video is set at "Le Bal de Magic City." It's all tuxedos, tiaras, martini glasses, and feather boas in the style of Paris nightlife. Just as Watley's video reveals the postcard-perfect world of the supper club to be a temporary fantasy, O'Connor's performance at the ball throws into relief how a love song itself is a respite from reality and a meditation on possibility.

Those fairytale experiences of attending a ball (or at least a dance club that calls itself one) can be real, of course. A dreamy night out, especially one where we hear an emotionally charged song, can become a flashbulb memory that stays with us for a lifetime. And the club where couples slow-dance to O'Connor's crooning may reflect what would have been Porter's lived experience. In the video (directed by John Maybury), flappers sway with each other and so do sailors as they orbit the center of the dance floor amidst a crowd of otherwise gender-mixed couples. Rather than reflecting a 1990s political agenda (as the network producer feared), the moment simply invokes the permissive culture of 1920s Paris that Porter would have enjoyed. It was a city where "homosexuals and homosexual relationships were accepted, if not always with enthusiasm, at least with a shrug, in a Paris where homosexuality had not been banned since the Revolution."[8] O'Connor doesn't care who is dancing with whom. She's up there on stage, barely recognizable in a long blonde wig, singing wistfully into the microphone (Figure 4.1.)

For all the ways it sounds like a familiar jazz standard, this "You Do Something to Me" represents a departure from its original version. O'Connor takes what was originally a duet between flirting lovers and turns it into an expression of solitary longing. The original version was the lead number in Porter's first full musical *Fifty Million Frenchmen* (1929). In

Figure 4.1 Sinéad O'Connor, "You Do Something to Me (*Red Hot + Blue*)" (Dir. John Maybury, Chrysalis Records, 1990), screenshot from the music video.

the original production, the song was performed as a duet by Genevieve Tobin and William Gaxton, playing the roles of Looloo Carroll and Peter Forbes. Forbes falls in love with Carroll at first sight, and he bets his best friend that he can woo her without revealing that he's swimming in money. In the original, love is a contest, a jest, a game. In O'Connor's version, love is expressed to someone physically absent but present in the singer's mind. It's that state of romantic love which relies on memory of the last encounter and the anticipation of the next one. It's that way in which love is so often, as Shakespeare's Sonnet 129 captures nicely, "before, a joy proposed; behind, a dream." The fact that the singer is lost in this song, while the dancing couples are too, reminds us of the adaptability of these love songs. While some listeners might be politically invested in the idea that classic love songs can only celebrate heterosexual love, the reality of the gender-free pronouns in Porter's lyrics is that each listener can imagine themselves in the place of the sung-to or the singer, as the "you" who does something magical or the "me" who experiences that magic. And the lone singer underscores that this type of idealized love might find its purest expression during absence.

The club. The music. Dance hall days. The intimacy, even in a room full of strangers, that a club can offer. The happened-upon tune. The kismet of a surprising song lyric, a familiar face at a nearby table, or eyes locking during a meaningful refrain. Porter's songs create such spaces in the mind and in the moment. But in January of 1942, Porter—with financial support from a group of friends—actually did create one of those physical spaces. He opened the 1-2-3 Club at 123 East 54th Street in New York City.[9] It was a spot with a piano player and customers gathered around tables chatting or playing gin rummy in a large, low-ceilinged, softly lit room. It also functioned as a safe gathering place for gay people. On September 14, 1942, Porter invited Nelson Barclift to meet him there:

COME TO "123" TONITE = COLE.[10]

The invitation at once sounds like code and is as straightforward as it seems. It's playful, and it's musical when we think of musicians setting the tempo before beginning to play.

And such safe spaces were much needed, but bars and performance halls were also spaces that came under efforts by the government to silence gay people or render them invisible. In 1927, the New York state legislature prohibited any play from "depicting or dealing with, the subject of sex degeneracy, or sex perversion." In 1940, the New York City police began requiring nightclub employees to undergo a fingerprint check as part of the prohibition of employment to people "who *pretended to be* homosexual or those who were homosexual."[11] It's no wonder, then, that both O'Connor and Watley choose the dancehall or nightclub as the setting for their videos. These are worlds-within-worlds that promise escape from judgmental eyes.

But the entirety of the video for "You Do Something to Me" is not in that 1920s Paris nightclub. It ends by showing O'Connor as fans would think of her, with her characteristically shaved head. She's in the present now, and so are we, as we see her holding a candle at an AIDS vigil. The song becomes not just one of longing but of mourning for those who have been lost. It's still a song of love, but it's also a call to action. The "You" who does something to the singer may be a lover with whom she wants to live a life. Or it may be a deceased loved one who inspires her to take action. Or it may be "you," the listener, whom she loves even if she doesn't know you, for whom she is willing to fight. In other words, the Sinéad O'Connor who ends this video announces herself as a member of an army of lovers.

And in that moment, she's wearing a t-shirt adorned with artwork that was part of the larger *Red Hot + Blue* project. It's designed by Jenny Holzer and has one of my all-time favorite legends composed by the artist (Figure 4.2).

It simply reads:

IN A DREAM YOU SAW A WAY TO SURVIVE AND YOU WERE FULL OF JOY

What is the dream that promises survival? In the case of O'Connor's "You Do Something to Me," it's not a vision

Figure 4.2 Sinéad O'Connor, "You Do Something to Me" (*Red Hot + Blue*) (Dir. John Maybury, Chrysalis Records, 1990), screenshot from the music video.

of the future but rather a vision of the past. But maybe that's what nostalgia is: a vision for a desired outcome that can only stem from a mental image of a historical past as we fantasize it had once been. Our longing for the past is a wish for how things might be in the future. Politically, this can be something conservative: "Make America Great Again." But with love songs, it's about a return to some originary point in our romantic evolution. The way to survive is not lost to some bygone era but a return to the dream itself that has so occupied people across eras. The promise of love, but not just of finding someone to love and be loved by. It's the promise of loving oneself. Of experiencing a kind of wholeness.

It's the past that reassures us that we can survive and that holds the promise of future joy. Porter's songs comfort us by giving us something we can strive for, an encounter with love in a world with a virus, in a time after loss. This is what history does for us, and it's why LGBTQ+ history is so important. It's why queer history is a matter of survival. To showcase gay lives in the past is to emphasize that same-sex desire has always had its place in the universal experience of love. At the same time, tracing such histories lets you know that others have loved like you do. And others will continue to love like you do.

Knowing that you have a history can help you see that you have a future.

Notes

1. Qtd. in *The Poets of Tin Pan Alley: A History of America's Great Lyricists* (2nd edn.), ed. Philip Furia and Laurie J. Patterson (Oxford: Oxford University Press, 2022 [1990]), 311.

2. Stephen Holden, "Why Cole Porter Prevails—Be It Pop, Rock or Even Rap," *The New York Times* (October 21, 1990): 34H.

3. Jody Watley, "Happy 30th Anniversary—Red Hot & Blue A Monumental First. The First Sensible Shame-Free Pop Culture Response to HIV/AIDS" (September 25, 2020). Accessed October 3, 2023. https://jodywatley.net/2020/09/25/happy-30th-anniversary-red-hot-blue-a-monumental-first-the-first-sensible-shame-free-pop-culture-response-to-hiv-aids/

4. This condition may only have been the estate's initial reaction to the project. John Carlin does indeed talk about Porter as a gay man in the album liner notes and says he would not have done so if the estate had not eventually said it was okay. John Carlin, interview by John S. Garrison, October 2, 2023.

5. *The Poets of Tin Pan Alley,* 312.

6. George Chauncey, *Gay New York: Gender, Urban Culture, and the Making of the Gay Male World, 1890–1940* (New York: Basic Books, 1994), 288.

7. Jody Watley, "World AIDS Day: *Red Hot + Blue* Looking Back" (December 1, 2017). Accessed October 3, 2023. https://jodywatley.net/2017/12/01/world-aids-day-red-hot-and-blue-looking-back/

8. Les Négresses Vertes's version of "I Love Paris" also nods to the free-love environment of France, as the video places it in Paris with a romantic encounter between an American man and a French woman. It's sung in multiple languages, and it

might be seen as a nod to Porter's own time in Paris and also a reminder that love often starts in a romantic elsewhere or elsewhen. Mary McAuliffe, *When Paris Sizzled: The 1920s Paris of Hemingway, Chanel, Cocteau, Cole Porter, Josephine Baker, and Their Friends* (New York: Rowman & Littlefield, 2016), 70.

9. It was during college that Porter became acquainted with New York City's vibrant nightlife, taking the train there for dinner, theater, and nights on the town with his classmates, before returning to New Haven, Connecticut, early in the morning.

10. "14 September 1942: Cole Porter to Nelson Barclift," *Letters*, 172.

11. Chauncey, *Gay New York*, 352.

5

I'm Yours

So many of the artists on *Red Hot + Blue* celebrate sadness, that mournful quality often shared by songs that lament lost love as well as songs that describe being in love. In my own life, I've often only realized that I am in love when I experience distance from the beloved. That separation makes me realize how much I need that particular person's companionship. And even when I'm with someone I love, I can experience a flash of loss when I realize how vulnerable I would be if the person was not there. Maybe it's here, among those maudlin songs on the album where it, and I, might feel the most *blue*. Ralph Ellison defines "the blues as a form that is an autobiographical chronicle of personal catastrophe expressed lyrically."[1] I even hear that sense of catastrophe when I listen to the album's songs that are not overtly about loss. Even in those songs where love is fully in the present, loss seems to lurk around their edges. Maybe that's because this is an album focused on AIDS. Or maybe it's because love itself thrives when it's most precarious and when it makes us profoundly aware of our own vulnerability.

So in Love

Like other contributors to *Red Hot + Blue,* k.d. lang delivers her song in a style that would be recognizable to Porter's original audience. The bossa nova rhythm links with her distinctive vocals to generate a richness that celebrates the beauty of "So in Love" while also capturing the melancholy of the story it chronicles. "Even without you," the singer pines, "my arms fold about you." She laments being deserted but admits that this void fuels her desire. It makes her so, so in love.

Watley's video placed her in a bygone era and O'Connor's situated her in the present but only in the final moment, but lang's video occurs fully in the present moment. Yet it's more nuanced than that. lang finds herself curiously perched between her personal past and her personal present. We encounter her in the aftermath of her lover's death from AIDS, yet she's telling us about the closeness she feels to her lover and about a deep sense of fullness she feels in her state of being deeply in love. As lang dismantles the paraphernalia needed for hospice care in her home, we realize that she perceives her lover as still there although her body has been physically removed. She's wearing rubber gloves, wheeling away an IV drip, putting away a chair used for assistance in the shower, and washing clothes in steaming hot water. She's clearing out her lonely house that's been turned into a care facility.

All that emphasis on hygiene, on barriers, on precaution. I suppose my first real boyfriend was a man named Roberto. This is in 1990. We'd practice the most cautious of sex.

I mean: nothing even remotely risky. It was awkward, choreographed, chaste. Afterward, he'd go into the bathroom for thirty, sometimes forty-five, minutes. I'd hear him washing and washing. We were both HIV-negative. But he'd already lost two gay brothers to AIDS. And his mother had this idea that two gay men could produce HIV just by having sex with each other. "She's not exactly wrong," Roberto would say. I never understood what he meant—dismissing it as a kind of paranoia in which we were all gripped—but I understand now, thinking about this video for "So in Love." In 1990, the test was only so accurate because one had to wait for antibodies to appear. And sometimes you heard that antibodies could remain undetectable for years. Or who knew what tragedy might yet come along for the gay community. But now I see Roberto and his mother's concerns as less about science or about group loss and more about the virus bringing to light our own endemic fears about losing the ones we love. And how vulnerable love makes us when we worry we might hurt someone we love. Being so in love means we might get hurt, and the threat of HIV infection added a new layer to that age-old risk.

As I wait in bed for Roberto, so much transpires within this moment. There is Roberto, who is in the bathroom worrying that one of us might become infected. There is me, who sits in bed not in the afterglow of some idyllic romantic encounter but in the wake of history. Roberto's personal history is that he's experienced the trauma of losing his only two siblings to the virus. And I'm in love for the first time, and it's nothing like those romantic preconceptions we have from books, movies, and songs like those of Cole Porter.

It's a confrontation with all the fear of gay relationships and the internalized disgust that Roberto's mother (and that Roberto) can't help but inherit despite my insistence to him that it's nonsense in the face of science. And I'm also sitting in a bedroom with the real fear of a disease that seems to be destroying the community into which I find myself coming out.

In her video for "So in Love," k.d. lang appears to be experiencing her loss by herself. But the lyrics keep insisting that she's not alone. As long as she can think about her lover, the feelings of love are still there. She has her memories, and these are enough to keep her company. The song and the video, then, are making a vital distinction. She was able to be in full couplehood with her lover but that did not involve transmission of the disease. Love can feel like a virus, and I often find myself saying to friends, "You just have to get it out of your system" or "you have to get that person out of your system." So that's made literal in the video. The character cannot get her lover out of her system emotionally but takes great care with sanitation to be sure that the lover does not enter her system in a virological sense. This distinction is subtle in the video, as is the notion that we're seeing the postscript to a same-sex relationship. As Carlin remarked to me recently, queer people could look for and pick up on the narrative as one about two women who were in love. Other listeners could see it as a more general caregiver story.[2]

k.d. lang was not out at the time but did not hesitate to follow director Percy Adlon's vision for the video of a woman who loses her lover to AIDS. In a recent interview where she was asked about the video, lang remarks,

It was really about the aftermath of the AIDS experience, and we wanted to portray a same-sex situation where my lover had passed away. And so, there was really no need in taking this song and trying to make it original or trending or anything. We just wanted to convey the emotion and the empathy of understanding that this disease has serious and dire consequences.[3]

The video thus showcases that loss is experienced by everyone. This humanizes the person with AIDS and the sexual minority. And it speaks to why anyone—whether they've experienced love or not—can listen to a Cole Porter tune and tap into its heights of joy or depths of sorrow. And perhaps it's true that queer loss, specifically in the face of AIDS or in the context of a pre-Stonewall society that associates same-sex love with mental disease and prosecutes such love as a crime, offers a case study for loss in its most acute form.

In the Still of the Night

I have always loved "In the Still of the Night." I have no idea when I first heard it, but for as long as I can remember it has always seemed such a powerful song because it meditates on the very nature of a love song. The "still of the night" is the actual time being described by the singer, when it is possible to simply think upon the beloved without interruption. And I think this "still" is also the moment for us, the listeners, to simply sit with the song and the emotion it evokes. In many ways, this song shares a close kinship with "Night and Day." In both, the lyrics describe thinking upon the beloved from the space of a lonely room. In both, the song is about the way those thoughts will repeat. In both, the song itself is a form of company for the solitary lover. In the context of the AIDS epidemic, the Neville Brothers's "In the Still of the Night" especially invites us to imagine time standing still. Like "So in Love," the song expresses a fantasy of holding the absent beloved in an embrace. When doing so, the lover thinks of a previous night where they embraced and imagining a time when they will embrace again. Here, in the still of the night again when dawn is about to break and the space of fantasy will be interrupted, there is that irksome sense that the previous embrace might be the last one.

"In the Still of the Night" itself allows the singer and the listener to suspend time. It feeds our hope that the lover might be present again and forestalls a moment when we might realize that this is impossible. Aaron Neville pines, "So before the light/Hold me again," knowing that this could be last time they meet in the still of the night. I think this is what Duke Orsino means in that opening line of *Twelfth Night:* "If music be the food of love, play on."[4] When the song brings the beloved back to us, even just in memory, we don't want the song to end. If the song ends, that means the love might never return.

The Neville Brothers's video was directed by Jonathan Demme. He had made several films, but his clearest link to the music world would be directing *Stop Making Sense* (1984), the Talking Heads concert film which won the

National Society of Film Critics Award for best documentary. I watched it again in its re-release this year. It's stunning. It's a masterpiece. Yet Demme, for me, will always be the director of *The Silence of the Lambs* (1991). A masterpiece in its own way, perhaps, but it's also a film which would make him a charged figure in terms of his relationship to the gay community.[5] It depicted a deranged killer who murdered women in order to use their skin to help transform him into a woman. It was hard not to see that character as reinforcing a long history of depictions of gay or transgender people as psychotic killers from *Psycho* to *Dressed to Kill*.

In 1993, Demme would release *Philadelphia*, one of the first major motion pictures to grapple with the AIDS epidemic. The film was a landmark in bringing AIDS to the foreground, starring Tom Hanks as a gay man suing his law firm for unjustly firing him for his sexual orientation and for having AIDS. Denzel Washington portrayed his attorney who must overcome his own homophobia and fear of the disease. Awareness of the film would be bolstered by Bruce Springsteen's title song, "Streets of Philadelphia," which reached number nine on the *Billboard* Hot 100, and it won the Academy Award for Best Original Song and four Grammy Awards, including Song of the Year. I remember people saying that *Philadelphia* was Demme's attempt to redeem himself after *The Silence of the Lambs,* but it didn't make a difference to me.

Now, as I realize that the director was part of the *Red Hot + Blue* project, I find myself reconsidering my too-easy dismissal of someone I don't even know.

I've Got Somebody Waiting

It occurs to me that "In the Still of the Night" could be considered an aubade, that particular kind of poetry where the speaker says goodbye to a lover in the morning. The words are often spoken in bed, when the lover wishes for just a moment longer with the beloved. It's often a secret love affair. The song, too, invokes that moment of aubade in *Romeo and Juliet* where one lover says he hears the lark heralding the morning and the other says it is just a nightingale signaling they have more time together.

As I write about these songs on *Red Hot + Blue,* I realize that so many of them describe romantic love not as an abiding experience but as a deeply precarious one. The experience of love is deepened not by a reassurance of *forever* but by a sense that those heights of joy could end at any moment. To be in love in these songs is to ride on the crest of a wave, never knowing if one might climb even higher but always knowing there must at some point be a crash upon the shore.

Most of Porter's love letters did not survive. Yet even a small sampling of the notes he did write (in French) to the dancer Boris Kochno in the 1920s find the familiar tones of anguish and need that we hear in the songbook. Listen to Cole write to Boris,

> Now that you've left, I'm trying to console myself by thinking of your return, but it's quite difficult. And the only thing that I really want to do, is to climb to the top of the Campanile and announce to the piazza that I'm in love to the point of dying with someone who has

taken this evening's train to Naples and that I'm going to follow him.[6]

I hear this, and it's all there for me. They've said goodbye, and it feels like they die a little. He wants to call out for his beloved but he can't speak about the love they share. All he can do is think of him.

It's so simple, really. The desire to reconnect becomes expectation, becomes anticipation. It's the reunion that will bring Cole back to life. Until then, it's the recollection of their previous union that keeps him going. The only way for him to imagine a way forward, a future, is to picture their past time together:

Oh there's nothing to say, Boris, I love you so much that I think only of you—I see only you and I dream only of the moment when we'll be reunited.

Goodnight, darling.[7]

These letters suggest that Porter's creative output comes from his romantic suffering, but couldn't we also say that he simply experiences the world so deeply that the truth of those feelings fuels his music? Porter is up at two o'clock in the morning. He's writing songs and he's writing to Boris in the still of the night:

But Boris—

It's getting difficult. All night I lay awake, thinking of you. And, all day, I was in Antwerp, even before you, to see you arrive. And tonight, you asked me why I have such preoccupied air—but this is all very serious. I don't hide it well + and if it continues I'd be really foolish. We went to the theatre this evening + and instead of watching the piece I watched you, all the time—I didn't listen to anything, I was before you, you smiled at me, you spoke to me, but it's folly, isn't it?

Ah Boris, how you have complicated my life!

And how happy I am, mon petit.

C.[8]

He's thinking of Boris night and day. He's trying to hide it but he can't. He's in love. He's so in love. And then it's all folly, but that just makes him happier. It's a state of precarity Cole longs for but cannot bear. It's that state of precarity that lets him know it's true love.

Wait for the Moon

Porter's personal life and his songs are driven by a sense of how powerful our desire for reunion can be, especially because it's subtended by a fear that reunion may not occur. And this makes concrete for me why he and his songs are such a perfect match for an album in response to the AIDS crisis. So many of my friendships in the 1990s with other gay men were haunted by a sense that we might not see each other again. And, if we did, that one of us might have since learned that we were HIV-positive or might now be experiencing symptoms of AIDS. My personal relationships were tinged with a sense of erosion because someone in my social network might become sick or die and because this was often the topic of conversation when catching up with friends. It made reunions with people just a bit more joyous, and it made news of emerging treatments crucial to the promise that those who were infected might get healthier.

This phantom sense of slow-moving catastrophe and its attendant hope for restoration is crystallized for me in the final scene of *Longtime Companion* (1989). The three main characters—Willy (played by Campbell Scott), his boyfriend Fuzzy (Stephen Caffrey), and their friend Lisa (Mary-Louise Parker)—walk together on a wintry beach. One thing I love about the scene is that Fuzzy is wearing a Gran Fury "Read My Lips" t-shirt.

It's Fire Island, where the film began when these three were surrounded by friends during a summer just before they'd read about a new cancer affecting gay men. They'd experienced the very beginning of the epidemic together, and each has lost many people close to them. Willy, Fuzzy, and Lisa have become activists, legal aid volunteers, and caregivers. The conversation on that foggy morning goes like this:

Willy: It seems inconceivable, doesn't it? That there was ever a time before all this, when we didn't wake up every day wondering, "Who's sick now? Who else is gone?"

Fuzzy:	Do you ever wonder if they ever do find a cure, people would go back to sleeping around?
Willy:	Who cares, you know?
Fuzzy:	It's just a question.
Willy:	I know. I know, but ... I'm sorry. I just think that ... whether people do or don't sleep around or what they do, it's just not the point. I'm sick of hearing people pontificate about it.
Lisa:	Except us.
Willy:	Except us. Exactly. I just wanna be there, if they ever do find a cure.
Fuzzy:	Can you imagine what it'd be like?
Lisa:	Like the end of World War Two.[9]

Music then rises up and a crowd comes running onto the beach. There's sunshine, and everyone is wearing bright pastels. People are laughing and they're hugging each other (Figure 5.1). Slowly, we realize that these are people who have died of AIDS. Characters from the film appear, in the reverse order of when they've died, all the way back to the first friend we met, who was one of the first people with AIDS. He had been terrified and alone in a hospital bed with a disease no one could identify. But now he's healthy and he's happy.

It's a scene of reunion and restoration, of going back. When Lisa says, it'll be "like the end of World War Two," it sets us up for that streaming crowd of people celebrating. In a larger sense, that reference to the war underscores that a cure for HIV disease would mean the end of the threat

Figure 5.1 *Longtime Companion* (Dir. Norman René, Samuel Gold-wyn Films, 1990), screenshot from the film.

of new deaths. We get a glimpse of a time when people can celebrate with each other and love without fear. In a smaller and more intimate sense, Lisa's wish is one for the resurrection of loved ones needlessly lost. The film doesn't let us stay in the fantasy, though. The final minutes of *Longtime Companion* show us the backs of the three friends walking away from us. It's winter again, and they've all gone silent, deep in their thoughts. They can't know if that prediction they've imagined will ever come.

Willy, Fuzzy, and Lisa are in that same space of waiting that we found Sinéad O'Connor at the end of "You Do Something to Me." They all hover in the wake of a dream about a future where they were full of joy, but they know that vision is built on nostalgia for what they wish it was like in the past.

Notes

1. Ralph Ellison, "Richard Wright's Blues," in *Living with Music: Ralph Ellison's Jazz Writings*, ed. Robert G. O'Meally (New York: The Modern Library, 2002), 103.

2. John Carlin, interview by John S. Garrison, October 2, 2023.

3. Christianne Amanpour, "Interview with John Carlin and k.d. lang," *CNN* (December 1, 2020). Accessed November 1, 2023. http://edition.cnn.com/TRANSCRIPTS/2012/01/ampr.01.html

4. William Shakespeare, *Twelfth Night, or, What You Will*, ed. Barbara A. Mowat and Paul Werstine (New York: Washington Square Press, 1993), 1.1.1.

5. *The Silence of the Lambs* won Academy Awards in all five major five categories: Best Picture, Best Director, Best Actor, Best Actress, and Best Adapted Screenplay.

6. Porter's letters and telegrams to Kochno are handwritten in imperfect French, and the editors have polished the language in their translations. We don't know if responses from Kochno ever existed. The editors note that most of the letters are undated and thus their chronology was reconstructed based on Porter's travels and references within the letters. "[?September 6, 1925]: Cole Porter to Boris Kochno," *Letters*, 55.

7. "[?September 6, 1925]: Cole Porter to Boris Kochno," *Letters*, 55.

8. "[probably late September 1925]: Cole Porter to Boris Kochno," *Letters*, 64.

9. *Longtime Companion*. Directed by Norman René (Los Angeles, CA: Samuel Goldwyn Company, 1989). DVD.

6

Anything Goes

Commentators on *Red Hot + Blue* often struggled with the sheer variety of styles and tones on the album. For example, one reviewer found himself confronted with "an overwhelming diversity of musical treatments— with performances running the gamut from the faithful to the unrecognizable."[1] Another reviewer felt that "we're too distracted for any point to be conveyed [so that] *Red Hot & Blue* is a mixed bag."[2] The album does give us a jarring range of moods, but this strikes me as consistent with the sense of the dismay that accompanies love in the time of AIDS. Indeed, a confused state may mark all forms of heightened desire as it is always haunted by the danger of pending loss and future mourning. We hear this in a quick brushstroke in the way Porter signed that letter to his lover who has left him alone, "Ah Boris, how you have complicated my life! And how happy I am, mon petit."[3]

Just One of Those Things

The mixing of emotions and genres is perhaps most in our face when Kirsty MacColl and the Pogues combine "Miss Otis Regrets" and "Just One of Those Things." The lyrics depict love-gone-wrong that leads to murderous rage, all in the context of a list of famous lovers whose affairs end in demise. The two songs come together to create a dialogue between disillusioned lovers in a manic, Celtic blend of folk and punk. This recording subverts the smooth lyricality of earlier versions of Porter's songs, but it's true to the contemporary artists' styles and I believe appropriate for the nature of *Red Hot + Blue*.

Charles Schwartz, one of Porter's many biographers, notes how hard it is to "reconcile Cole's unmistakable maudlin streak [with] his even more pronounced unsentimental one." Schwartz also notes how Porter's unadulterated sincerity might be "especially surprising in one normally considered the personification of worldliness, savoir-faire, and even cynicism."[4] The video for the mash-up of "Miss Otis Regrets" and "Just One of Those Things" (directed by Neil Jordan, who would shortly thereafter direct the films *Interview with the Vampire* and *The Crying Game*) itself intermingles various forms of dancing: flamenco, waltz, vaudeville, swing, and traditional Irish dance. There is a kinetic scene of movement and mixture of artists and genres. It's raucous and loud and emphasizes what a mish-mash the Porter songbook is and what mixed emotions collide when love and mourning overlap.

Well, Did You Evah!

MacColl and The Pogues stage a scene that's anything but those quiet clubs where Watley and O'Connor crooned. Those two other videos seemed more in line with the ritzy, debonair settings where one might imagine Porter being seen or his music being played. Think of his 1956 film *High Society* which starred Bing Crosby, Grace Kelly, and Frank Sinatra. In some ways, the movie's pure Porter. Crosby and Sinatra, with their tuxedos and their cocktails in a gentlemen's library with a ballroom outside. They're singing. They're dancing. If you didn't know better, you'd think they were a gay couple. And the song they're singing is one of the greats: "Well, Did You Evah!"

When viewers encountered Debbie Harry and Iggy Pop doing their rendition of "Well, Did You Evah!" in the television special, they'd first been shown an old film of the *High Society* premier, including Cole Porter's arrival at the theater and a clip from the film itself with Crosby and Sinatra. As the reel transitions into the two modern performers strutting through run-down city streets, we're invited to see it as simultaneously a parody and an homage to that old film. The two are dressed in a ball gown and a tuxedo and singing about French champagne. But they're stumbling into a liquor store in Jersey City during broad daylight and buying dog food. Later, they're clumsily trying to rob a bank.

The video is directed by Alex Cox, who wanted it to feel "anarchic."[5] In a documentary about the making of the album, Harry suggests that she and Pop are "survivors" of rough times who feel they can speak to those trying to survive this latest crisis. She expresses hope that *Red Hot + Blue* will spur people to discuss sexuality openly and "get over the fixation on reproduction" as the only goal for sex. Pop agrees when he describes the goal to "lighten up and make a more tolerant atmosphere."[6] So, they're poking fun at the stodgy rules of that high society that belongs to the ritzy New York and Paris that we might think of Cole Porter being part of. In some ways, they're revealing that both the clothes and the songs are a form of drag anyone can put on.

That was part of the message of Jennie Livingston's 1990 film *Paris Is Burning*. With footage and interviews collected from the mid- to late-1980s, the film documented the black drag ball culture in New York City. In some ways, the performers revealed the artifice of gender and class differences by deftly impersonating forms of both. But, as bell hooks has remarked, the film is simultaneously "perpetuating the fantasy that ruling-class white culture is the quintessential site of unrestricted joy, freedom, power, and pleasure."[7] Her observation reminds us that there is a level of privilege in Harry and Pop's ability to pretend to dress up and dance around without a care in the world.

But public performance that breaks norms around expected behavior is more dangerous for some than for others. Around the time of my writing this book, O'Shae Sibley, a 28-year-old black gay man, was stabbed to death because he was vogueing in a gas station when a Beyoncé song came on.[8] Men attacked him, hurling gay slurs and telling him to stop dancing like that. The fantasy of Iggy Pop and Debbie Harry's video is, in part, just that: a fantasy.

People risk their lives if they break expected norms in public. And such behaviors are especially dangerous when racism and homophobia are in the mix.

It's Alright with Me

I am moving quickly here through the discussion of these songs because it underscores the at-times vexing range of tone on the album. Choosing another track, we might find ourselves next at Tom Waits's "It's Alright With Me," another opportunity to meditate on the mix of emotion in the album, in Porter's life, and in the AIDS pandemic. The video is directed by Jim Jarmusch, whom viewers would know from the indie black-and-white comedies *Strangers in Paradise* (1984) and *Down by Law* (1986). Waits's performance blends rock and blues in a way that might sound alien to both genres. The inherent strangeness of the rendition and the video speak to Waits's signature experimental style: raspy vocals and other-wordly dancing that illustrates his debt to vaudeville.

Waits's experience with the *Red Hot + Blue* project initiated his now long history of utilizing the power of music for social change. His trajectory thus ties to Bono's, in terms of how the album instigated his involvement with global AIDS activism. As I will discuss in the next chapter, Annie Lennox's long-time commitment to fighting the disease also began with her work on the album. So *Red Hot + Blue* was the start of the Red Hot phenomena but it was also an inspiration for individual artists to become involved for the long term. After his song for Red Hot, Waits went on to perform at benefits for gay rights. He has also performed at awareness- and fund-raising events for those affected by the L.A. riots of the early 1990s as well as for Hope House, National Fundraising Day of Action, Murder Victims' Families for Reconciliation, and others.[9] Working on the album seems to have helped him understand how music, with all its propensity to stir a range of reactions across diverse listeners, has a special capacity for affecting change.

Who Wants to Be a Millionaire?

Porter's "Who Wants to Be a Millionaire?" was given a techno re-imagining by Thompson Twins. One of two songs not to have an accompanying video (the other being "Love for Sale" by Fine Young Cannibals), the song nonetheless offers an opportunity to reflect on the complexities of love that are explored in songs throughout *Red Hot + Blue*. The lyrics run through a list of things a millionaire would have: a yacht, a country estate, an opera box, a fancy car, and so on. But the respondent says that all they want is their beloved. Carlin writes, "the music in this album revives Porter's work, virtually for the first time in the Rock era, […] because it contains a message we need to be reminded of in these difficult times."[10] Thompson Twins's choice of song does this especially, I think, because it emphasizes that times of crisis can reinforce the value of emotional ties over material goods.

When we hear the song, it might be easy to dismiss its sentiment by noting that Porter himself was a millionaire.

Having money, though, is not a reprieve from unhappiness. Of a 1940s biopic about Porter, Orson Welles once quipped, "'What will they use for a climax? The only suspense is: will he or won't he accumulate $10 million?'"[11] I think it's important not to dismiss Porter's unhappiness in light of his upper-class status. At the same time, we should not assume that he was solely a tragic figure. It seems absurd now, but I remember when the Names Project AIDS Memorial Quilt came to my college campus in 1990. The coordinator of the event was a small man with a mustache who I assumed to be gay. He wore a black suit for all three days that the quilt was displayed on campus. I vividly remember wondering if he always wore the suit, if he was permanently in mourning. And I wondered if many gay men were like this: always sad and always thinking about the many people they had lost to AIDS. As I reduced my understanding of gay people to one of a community permanently in the wake of loss, was I not projecting my own fears of how my own life would be defined?

Down in the Depths

Lisa Stansfield's rendition of "Down in the Depths" exemplifies Porter's maudlin streak. The singer is high above it all, contemplating suicide from a ninetieth-floor window. She admits, "I'm deserted and distressed/In my regal-eagle mess." Her heart's below the ground already, and the plunge would match the current state of her spirits. Porter upends his usual depiction of penthouses as lofty sites of glitz to be cells of silence and despair. To look at the video, you wouldn't know it. Stansfield is accompanied by a big band orchestra and sings on a lighted stage reminiscent of the golden age of Broadway. But to listen to the lyrics and to look past the appearance of the singing socialite, we peer directly into the darkness that sometimes gripped the composer.

Porter may even have seen wealth as a burden. When he was young, he and his grandfather would go horse-back riding. As the two rode by the local poorhouse, Cole's grandfather would indicate the building with his riding crop and warn that if Cole did not work hard enough, he was destined to live there.[12] In fact, the wealthy grandfather urged Cole's parents to send their son to either business school or a military school in order to inherit the family business of land management and mining.[13]

And how much does money matter anyway when there is the looming possibility of catastrophe? In his letters, we hear that the composer feared being abandoned by the men he loved. But a catastrophe arrived for him not in the slow-motion collapse of heartbreak (though there was that as well) but in the form of the horse-riding accident that crushed Porter's legs in 1937. Porter was left disabled and in constant pain, but he continued to work. Eventually one of his legs needed to be amputated. Yet he used humor to manage pain. He gave the name "Geraldine" to his ruined right leg, and he christened his slightly better off left leg "Josephine." Nonetheless, as he suffered from sleeplessness caused by chronic pain, "the deterioration in the quality of Cole Porter's songs was due solely to his agonized physical condition."[14] Prior to the accident, Cole began to achieve success in the 1920s, and by the 1930s he was one of the leading songwriters for the Broadway musical stage. Unlike many successful Broadway composers, Porter wrote the lyrics as well as the music for his songs. But the accident interrupted that creative output and rise to fame.[15]

His wife Linda came home from Paris after the accident. She had been planning to file for divorce, but the accident brought her and Porter's mother Kate to his aid. Caregiving is a special kind of love, and Cole clearly valued all that Linda did for him. After her death, he had a rose named for her. The doctors initially advocated for amputation but Linda and Kate, following Cole's wishes, advocated that the legs be operated on instead. Specialists in New York were able to keep the need for amputation at bay for almost two decades. But the constant pain and reduced mobility left Cole down in the depths. Ethel Merman recalled that Porter lost his desire to keep living after one of his legs was eventually amputated.[16]

In the period where he reconciled to life with those crushed legs, things must have looked grim. In a letter to his old friend, theater and film actor Monty Woolley, Porter writes,

> If I had merely broken my legs, I'd have no complaints to make. But, although the left leg got a compound fracture, (that means that the bones went through the skin and were exposed to the air), the right leg was mashed to such a pulp from below the knee to the ankle that a great many of the nerves were injured, one of them very seriously

and most of the pain has come from there. From the second day it was obvious that the toes of my right leg were without sensation. And after a few more days, the excruciating pains, as if from burns, began.[17]

Here is where I hear the echoes of the complaints of friends who dealt with the effects of AIDS-related chronic pain from conditions such as peripheral neuropathy, that strange condition that alternates between hurting, tingling, and numbing.

The pain and the treatments made Porter more aware of his own mortality and again spun him through a range of emotions in quick succession. His letter continues,

Morphine simply made me want to give parties and did nothing toward diminishing the pain. Hyoscine drove me crazy, Nembutal … induced nothing but drowsiness. Then they hit on Dilaudid … it's a mixture of morphine with a lot of other nice drugs … I have had a shot of it every four hours for the last month and it has saved my life.[18]

Porter is jubilant but suffering. He's manic, he's mad, he's sleepy. It's awful, it's "nice," and the ultimate feeling is relief. Carlin's co-producer Leigh Blake had this to say about the goal of *Red Hot + Blue*, "We want to dress the word AIDS in a beautiful frame to help erase the stigma associated with the phrase."[19] The album succeeds at that in terms of its careful craft and inspiring sound. At the same time, close attention to the meanings of the songs, especially in the context of Porter's life, reveals the tragic underpinnings that drive the music to such beautiful heights.

To Follow Every Fancy

If it feels like the songs jump from message to message, from mood to mood, it's because they do. That's the feel of the album *as an album.* Another turn on a shuffle setting might take us to "Love for Sale" by The Fine Young Cannibals. The original version of the song was *the* signature hit from *The New Yorkers* (1930), though its lyrics and the idea that it was sung by a commercial sex worker led one reviewer at the time of its original release to dismiss it as "filthy."[20] Surely that signals why it belongs on the album. To talk about AIDS prevention, 1990s culture had to break through long-held taboos and get used to talking about sex in a way that might disturb more conservative listeners. "Love for Sale" is one of several songs on the album where Porter himself walked a fine line between too-clever puns and open discussion of sex. The original song was so explicit that it could not be played on the radio for years. The Federal Communications Commission (FCC) may have banned it from radio play at the time, but it still garnered significant record sales in the 1930s.

The song brings the lived experience of commercial sex workers into focus as lead singer Roland Gift voices a pimp attempting to sell two women to passing men. Porter's original language speaks explicitly to a population at high risk for the disease. But the ways in which we talk about—or won't talk about—love rarely operate in isolation. The history of this song, like other examples we've seen in this book, shows how music can dismantle or reinforce negative ideas about class, gender, and race. The composer himself made changes in the song to make it more palatable to his white audience. The commercial sex worker originally was white in *The New Yorkers,* but Porter altered the character to be a black person to play more directly into the stereotypes that would be legible to the show's upper-class white audience.[21]

Begin the Beguine

I'll end my shuffle through the tracks by just noting how Salif Keita's "Begin the Beguine" contributes to the dynamics I've been tracing in this book. His song brings a world music sound not only by being a non-Western artist but also by singing in his own native language. And for those of us who don't understand the words or don't know the original lyrics (both are true of me), we can still understand the feelings invoked by the song. The instrumental is fast-paced and joyous, but Keita's voice has that distinct sound in any language: longing. It feels like an expression of joy in the face of trauma and danger. That feeling is brought home by the way the video has a group of non-stop dancers surrounding the singer. Yet the background is a bright, luminescent red, and an illustration of Africa in flames intermittently flashes on screen.

Keita's video ends with information about HIV infections in Africa. "Begin the Beguine" is thus an admixture of emotions, nations, and messages. It's a well-needed nod on *Red Hot + Blue* to the global reach of the pandemic, which we also hear in the television special when John Malkovich urges, "I'm going to talk about sex. Go to the souk, casbah, pharmacist, and get condoms." The song and the comment increase awareness that people are also suffering and dying from the disease across other continents. It was about remembering the global connectedness that transports disease.

On the one hand, people in the major markets for the album and the television special, the United States and the UK, needed to be reminded of the global nature of the pandemic. On the other hand, there was a pernicious side to people's understanding of the flow of HIV across national borders. It may take a moment to remember how the history of HIV was shaped by an (now-debunked) idea that a "Patient Zero" could be blamed for the fast and widespread transmission early on.[22] Indeed, this patient zero narrative thrived on blame-and-shame dynamics that resound in the White House press conference or those jokes about AIDS. The story of a promiscuous gay man—a Canadian flight attendant no less—spreading the disease through his lust and lack of domestic grounding was just too tempting, too believable. Didn't he relentlessly have sex at every layover stop? Didn't he have hundreds of partners within the span of months? Didn't he continue to have sex even after he knew he was sick, even after he knew how the virus was transmitted?

To even feel like one should answer these questions is to ignore the set of beliefs behind them—about gay male promiscuity, about whether having multiple sexual partners itself is a vice, about the value of erotic connection in the absence of love—beliefs that themselves have been deeply encoded in our culture. The reality is, I think, that humans experience desire and love in complex ways that defy the simplistic moralizing that sought to regulate HIV funding and limit representations in prevention campaigns, all in service of a fiction of what is normal.

All of You

Acknowledging the jumble of emotions and experiences captured on the album is also to acknowledge Porter's life as a jumble.[23] To watch the two biopics about Porter, you would think he compartmentalized different aspects of his life. *Night and Day* (1946) is largely a fiction, with a robustly heterosexual Porter played by Cary Grant and Linda played by Alexis Smith. In *De-Lovely* (2014), Kevin Kline played Cole and Ashley Judd played Linda. The film is a fiction, too, but much more honest about his love of men. Still, the male lovers are a secret. Linda knows about them, but they're kept unsaid.

This does not actually seem to be the case when one reads Porter's letters. In 1918, he met Linda Lee Thomas, a rich, Louisville, Kentucky-born divorcée who, like Cole, loved to travel and entertain. She knew he was gay but they became loving companions, marrying in 1919. For Linda, the marriage offered continued social status and a partner who was the opposite of her abusive first husband. Cole and Linda remained married from December 19, 1919, until her death in 1954. Listen to Porter describe his early meetings with Linda. When Cole met Linda in 1918, he wrote to his friend Monty Woolley,

> I lunch and dine with Linda Thomas every day, and between times, call her up on the telephone. She happens to be the most perfect woman in the world and I'm falling so in love with her that I'm attractively triste.[24]

We will never know just how physical the relationship was, but we can recognize that "so in love" is the title of one of the love songs on *Red Hot + Blue*. And it's a phrase that can refer to the deepest friendship or romantic entanglements.

And it would be a mistake to place Porter's relationship with his wife at odds with his gay relationships. It's two o'clock in the morning "after a dull dinner, but a long one." Cole is missing Nelson Barclift, but he's also thinking about how he can make it work with numerous loves in his life. Linda has met Nelson recently, and Cole's urging him to like her as much as she likes him:

> I say good night to you now. If you have time, call up Linda at Williamstown, I know that the more you know her, the happier you will be […] and if you've got any spare days, ask her to ask you up. The reason I mention this is because I love you so much.[25]

There seems to be room in Porter's heart for both Nelson and Linda. He's hardly keeping them apart or keeping one a secret from the other. Instead, he offers proof of his love for Nelson by wanting him to be close to Linda.

We hear such sentiments again here in a letter to Boris Kochno, where the composer is pleased by the memory of an encounter between two people he loves:

> You made a great friend today—Linda. After everyone had left, she came to my room to see me and spoke to me only about you—she said you had been charming, that she found you very kind, and that you had laughed a great deal together this afternoon.[26]

There's such a simple sense of comfort to this letter. We don't hear the heartache that characterizes other letters to Boris. Indeed, the ease of the letter's tone matches the ease with which the composer would like his wife and his lover to get along. And then this follows in that same letter:

> I put the third phrase at the end of the list because I believe it is the most important as she finds very few people amuse her and, I do not know how to tell you how grateful I am—you did it. And that makes everything so much easier.[27]

When he writes, "that makes everything so much easier," it doesn't sound like Cole's hiding anything. In this last bit of the letter, he's genuinely glad that Linda's found someone who brings her happiness and the three of them might be happy in an unconventional unison.

Just like his songbook and just like *Red Hot + Blue,* Porter seems to have enjoyed encouraging people and desires, as well as styles and moods, to intermingle and overlap in a world where—for better or worse but hopefully ending up for the better—anything goes.

Notes

1. Katherine Bergeron, "Uncovering Cole," *Repercussions* 4.2 (1995): 28.

2. David Browne, "Red Hot & Blue," *Entertainment Weekly* (November 2, 1990). Accessed August 15, 2023. https://ew.com/article/1990/11/02/red-hot-blue-2/

3. "[probably late September 1925]: Cole Porter to Boris Kochno," *Letters,* 64.

4. Charles Schwartz, *Cole Porter* (New York: The Dial Press, 1977), 224.

5. "*Red Hot + Blue* Extras," *BBC* (posted to Vimeo on June 14, 2019). Accessed November 1, 2023. https://vimeo.com/342288595

6. "*Red Hot + Blue* Extras"

7. bell hooks, "Is Paris Burning?" in *Black Looks: Race and Representation* (New York: Routledge, 1992), 149.

8. Maria Cramer and Wesley Parnell, "Man Fatally Stabbed in Confrontation as He Danced at a Gas Station," *The New York Times* (July 31, 2023). Accessed October 10, 2023. https://www.nytimes.com/2023/07/31/nyregion/stabbing-gas-station-brooklyn.html

9. Barney Hoskyns, *Lowside of the Road: A Life of Tom Waits* (New York: Crown, 2009), 350 and 414–17.

10. John Carlin, liner notes, *Red Hot + Blue* (Chrysalis Records, 1990).

11. Qtd. in Todd S. Purdum, "Cole Porter's Two Biopics? They're Night and Day," *The New York Times* (June 20, 2014). Accessed October 1, 2023. https://www.nytimes.com/2004/06/20/

movies/film-cole-porter-s-two-biopics-they-re-night-and-day.
html

12. William McBrien, *Cole Porter: A Biography* (New York: Alfred
A. Knopf, 1998), 3–4.

13. McBrien, *Cole Porter: A Biography*, 19.

14. Alec Wilder, "Cole Porter (1891–1964)," in *American Popular
Song: The Great Innovators, 1900–1950*, ed. Robert Rawlins
(New York: Oxford University Press, 2022), 250.

15. Toward the end of his career, he made a massive comeback
with his most successful musical, *Kiss Me, Kate*, adapting *The
Taming of the Shrew* with such brilliance that it won the first
Tony Award for Best Musical in 1948. For me, *Kiss Me Kate*
itself is a reminder of hope's possible return.

16. Ethel Merman, *Merman* (New York: Simon and Schuster,
1978), 133.

17. "December 2, 1937: Cole Porter to Monty Woolley," *Letters,*
149–50.

18. "December 2, 1937: Cole Porter to Monty Woolley,"
Letters, 151.

19. Qtd. in Alan Light, "*Red Hot & Blue*: AIDS Benefit," *Rolling
Stone* (October 18, 1990): 22.

20. Frederick Nolan, "Cole Porter," in *Dictionary of Literary
Biography: Vol 265: American Song Lyricists, 1920–1960*,
ed. Philip Furia (Detroit, MI: Thomson Gale, 2002), 395.

21. McBrien, *Cole Porter: A Biography*, 137.

22. For an excellent study that dismantles this myth from
a biomedical perspective and also considers the social
implications of the myth's spread, see Richard A. McKay,

Patient Zero and the Making of the AIDS Epidemic (Chicago: University of Chicago Press, 2017).

23. Even his life story seems to be a mix of genres, even from the outset. He was classically trained in music at Yale, was involved in the glee club and the drama club, and would go on to receive further training in music in Paris. In 1917, when the United States entered the First World War, Porter moved to Paris and appears to have served in the French Foreign Legion. This claim has been called into question, but the Legion lists Porter as one of its soldiers and displays his portrait at its museum. He seems to have served in North Africa but also maintained a luxury apartment in Paris, where he entertained lavishly. He threw extravagant parties in spaces where fewer than 1,000 people would make the ballroom dance floor feel empty.

24. Cole Porter, "March 25, 1918: Cole Porter to Monty Woolley," in *The Letters of Cole Porter*, ed. Cliff Eisen and Dominic McHugh, New Haven: Yale University Press, 2019), 30.

25. "June 1, 1942: Cole Porter to Nelson Barclift," *Letters*, 170.

26. "[?September 6, 1925]: Cole Porter to Boris Kochno" *Letters*, 55.

27. "[?September 6, 1925]: Cole Porter to Boris Kochno," *Letters*, 55.

7

So Near and Yet So Far

I don't know if we'll reunite with lost loved ones after we die. I sure hope so. Sometimes it seems like we must. When my friend Chuck died from AIDS in 1999, I didn't find out until a few weeks afterward when a mutual friend told me. Chuck and I had worked together, but he went on disability leave when he was diagnosed with non-Hodgkin's lymphoma. We'd meet for coffee sometimes, but I'd seen him less and less frequently during those months when he was doing chemo. About a week or so after I'd heard the news, I was certain that I saw him walking about a block ahead of me on Castro Street. And, strangely, I wasn't surprised. I mean, he was a familiar figure in the neighborhood, often out walking or talking with guys on a street corner, or grabbing coffee at an outside table in order to just chat with whoever came by. When I saw him that day (or thought I saw him), I was certain then that I had mis-heard the news of his death, or even dreamed it.

Even after his death was confirmed by multiple people in our overlapping social circles, even after news went around at work, and even after I'd read his obituary in the local gay newspaper, I still felt certain that I'd seen Chuck on the street that day. Somehow, I knew that he was alive somewhere. Or, put a better way, I felt convinced that there was another world where Chuck was still alive. In some ways, that's the stuff of fantasy, I know, to think there are other worlds parallel to our own. But, for me, my abiding belief that Chuck is still alive somewhere is another way of saying that memory can be dizzying. It can make us lose our sense of up from down, forwards from backwards, anticipation from retrospect.

I think Hamlet feels this acutely after the death of his father. Even before his friend Horatio can tell him that he has seen the ghost of the recently departed king, the prince says,

HAMLET	My father!–methinks I see my father.
HORATIO	Where, my lord?
HAMLET	In my mind's eye, Horatio.
HORATIO	I saw him once; he was a goodly king.
HAMLET	He was a man, take him for all in all, I shall not look upon his like again.
HORATIO	My lord, I think I saw him yesternight.[1]

Which is more believable? That a son might have a loving remembrance of his father, who was imperfect yet left such an impression that the son still sees him clearly in his mind's eye as if he were still alive? Or that an apparition returns from the afterlife? For me, loving memory and a ghost are very much the same thing. My disbelief that Chuck was no longer part of the world stemmed from how powerful a force he had been in my life. And I had readied myself for his death so many times and then been so surprised (and, eventually, not surprised) to see him once more walking the streets of our neighborhood. I suppose that I had somehow said goodbye to him so many times that I decided he could never truly leave me.

When Love Comes Your Way

There's so much loss in Porter's music. Even when the songs are being silly or when they're relishing in the high life, there's always a sense that this is just a moment of coming up for air from being down in the depths. Yet, in those darkest of moments when the singer sits alone and wonders if love will return, there is a sense that the memory of having loved and having been loved is a form of company. And that experience seems to pervade Porter's lived experience as well. Consider this letter and think about how the absence of Boris makes the composer go to pieces:

> And since you left, six days ago, I've had only one letter. Don't bother telling me that you haven't had time, because I know perfectly well that if you wanted to, nothing would be easier. And I want to underline the fact that I'm becoming a bit furious about it. I miss you so much that I am falling apart + if this continues—this utter silence—I don't dare think what I could do. Oh, Boris, write me and tell me that you love me as much as I love you. You can't say it too often, because you are so far from me and it makes me so miserable.[2]

This letter puts me in the mind of so many of the songs. But maybe the one that registers the most is "In the Still of the Night." In this letter and in that song, the lover has never felt love so strongly as when the beloved is absent. And here, when Porter says he's "falling apart" and "miserable" as he hopes to hear that Boris loves him as much as he loves Boris, we know how this is going to end. And so does Porter. The fact that Boris can't say "I love you" often enough, that he hasn't written, that he's gone away. It seems like Porter must already have foreknowledge of their eventual break-up. Even when Boris was present, it sounds like he was already absent because he never reciprocated the depth of love Porter had for him.

Porter desires the impossible. A few days later, he's still writing and hopes for a rendezvous in Florence:

> I went to look for a letter at the post office but there was nothing. No doubt you didn't receive my itinerary in time. But I wait for the next with great impatience. Fortunately I've arranged to be in Florence on the 20th and 21st— perhaps the 22nd. I'm sure it will be very difficult to meet but in any case I will have the great luxury to look at those beautiful eyes of which I dream, night and day, my Boris. Goodnight + don't forget for an instant that I love you.
>
> Ravenna
>
> Wednesday evening
>
> C.[3]

He's making excuses now for Boris's lack of letters. The beloved probably did not receive the latest itinerary. Cole is hoping to see him on the 20th or the 21st. He'll even extend his visit to Florence a day, if it helps. But he's already giving Boris an excuse, saying he understands how difficult it is to meet. And that final sentiment. He dreams of Boris night and day. He implores Boris not to forget him for an instant, but the very request suggests Cole knows that the growing distance between them is more than physical.

Porter just wants to hear that he is loved. He finds himself writing again a few days later:

> Maybe this bothers you to tell me such things but that's what I ask of you. That's what I dream of. I am so hungry for that—that you tell me you love me + thousands of times so I can read the words you have written during the night when I suffer to have your lips against mine—your lips that I have kissed so often + so tenderly, my Boris.
>
> Write to me, at Travellers Club.
>
> 25 Avenue des Champs-Elysées.[4]

His wish for an expression of love is a dream, a hungry yearning that burns deep under the hide of him. But that recollection of those lips that once kissed. It's a fall into memory. It's a vision of a wished-for future that consists of a past that never was, a time when Boris used to be just as in love with Cole.

And then there's one last missive. Cole sends it only fifteen minutes after the two men separate:

> This—it's just a word simply to tell you that I just left you a quarter of an hour ago + and that I miss you—but tanto.

> And to apologize if I didn't turn off the light + take you in my arms + tell you that you are the only thing in the world that is dear to me. Goodnight, my Boris.[5]

Porter just wanted to look at Boris, to burn into his memory the image of the man he loved. He tells him that he's the dearest thing in the world to him and calls him "my Boris." It's so much of what we find in the songs on *Red Hot + Blue*. But perhaps it resonates closest with "After You, Who?" Without the singular beloved, Cole does not believe there is another man for him in the world and is not sure who he is without Boris.

Was it Porter's extreme devotion that drove Boris to keep his distance? It seems that Boris was also involved at the time with Hermann Oelrichs Jr., a friend of Porter's. On September 19, 1925, during the same weeks when Porter was writing the letters quoted above, Oelrichs writes this to Boris,

> I know that I write you too much. But I love you too much, my angel. I think of you too much. I want to see you too much and that is going to end badly. Because you will soon say—Enough! I've had enough.[6]

The letter says overtly what Porter's letters only hint at. Just as Cole interrupts his own letter with "tanto," Oelrich knows his love is too much. He knows Boris will soon say "enough," and he knows that it's all "going to end badly."

What these letters say to me is that the songs on *Red Hot + Blue* are not hyperbole. I imagine that, at some point in our lives, a lot of us have felt like Porter and Oelrichs do in these letters. Heartbreak plays out in lived experience as slow-moving catastrophe. Yet, a love song may distill such deep feeling into only a few minutes of lyrical expression. A song can reflect back to us how we feel when we need to make sense of our inner life. A song might, alternatively, draw us out of ourselves and out into the world for a while. Or it might plumb the depths of our hearts to make us aware of the feelings we don't want to feel.

We should not fault the men writing these letters to Boris for loving him as much as they do. I think it's tempting to read these letters as desperation, as clinging, as obsession. We could dismiss them or downplay them as the self-indulgent desire driving something akin to *Death in Venice*. But I think it's real for many different kinds of loves. Certainly, there's a unique isolation to being gay in Porter's era, and there still is one now if you're gay. It's especially true among older gay people, and it's also especially true among young gay people. These terms of desperation and hidden longing flow through queer love letters from the past. That phrase: "That is going to end badly." How many times have I been there myself? Desire intensifies with the increased probability of future loss. It's true for people throughout history, and especially for queer people. And I think there is truth in the idea that AIDS made real that fundamental fear.

A song can capture that, especially the final one on the album that I would like to discuss.

Every Time We Say Goodbye

Annie Lennox's contribution to *Red Hot + Blue* was her first foray as a solo artist. Although *Diva* would be her first solo album in 1992, "Every Time We Say Goodbye" was her first project without her longtime Eurythmics collaborator Dave Stewart. And it was her first real encounter with the epidemic, which in turn would lead to her decades-long AIDS activism. She recalls,

> It really goes back to the '80s, with Leigh Blake and the *Red Hot + Blue* project. That was the first musical project that was actually directly highlighting the situation of HIV and AIDS with different artists. And I recorded a version of "Every Time We Say Goodbye." And that was my first induction into AIDS, and I worked with Derek Jarman, who actually tragically passed away from HIV and AIDS-related illness. And he was the first person I met who was HIV positive, and that was very thought-provoking.[7]

The filmmaker Derek Jarman was supposed to direct her music video for the television special, but he couldn't complete the work because of being too sick. He did, however, include her version of the song in his film *Edward II* (1991) and Lennox appears briefly in that film. So, Lennox's version of "Every Time We Say Goodbye" ended up having several significant lives on screen. A video directed by Ed Lachman was included in the *Red Hot + Blue* special, and the song also appears in the 1992 romantic comedy *Prelude to a Kiss*. That film was directed by Norman René, who also directed *Longtime Companion*. He died of AIDS in 1996 at the age of forty-five. Jarman died of AIDS in 1994 at the age of fifty-two.

Jarman's *Edward II* adapts Christopher Marlowe's 1594 play for the screen, and it showcases the romantic relationship between the king and his favorite Piers Gaveston, just as the original play does, but with a crucial shift.[8] In Marlowe's version, the royal court objects strongly to the relationship because of the class differences between the two men. In Jarman's film, it is very much the same-sex nature of the relationship that so raises the ire of the court. In *Edward II*, the filmmaker retains the original language of the play but maps the narrative conflict onto the struggle for gay rights and efforts to raise awareness of the HIV/AIDS epidemic.

While Jarman's *Edward II* intermingles contemporary elements in its backdrop—an anti-government protest, a rugby game, modern clothing—with non-modernized language from Marlowe's play, the most startling intrusion of the present comes when Edward must say farewell to Gaveston as he is banished. While the two speak, music comes over the scene. We hear Lennox sing Cole Porter's "Every Time We Say Goodbye." At first, it seems that the song is only for our ears, cueing the audience to the mood and meaning of the interaction. Lennox does appear on screen but seems to be elsewhere, unconnected to the action of the play, the visual presence of the singer just another one of Jarman's unusual cinematic choices. And it's such an apt song for the moment between these two characters. After all, the song opens by telling us that "Every time we say goodbye, I die a little."

The idea that we experience dying every time we bid someone farewell is not a new idea. In the nineteenth century, the philosopher Arthur Schopenhauer wrote that "every parting gives a foretaste of death, every reunion a hint of the resurrection."[9] He so concisely captures how we experience loss and joy in the moment but also as echoes of previous experiences and practice for new ones. Every time we hear a song, we re-experience emotions we associate with it as well as memories, both personal and cultural, that the song evokes. A song is a memory but it's a prediction too. We hear a song and think about how we have felt and how we want to feel—or never want to feel again—in the future. And maybe this is even more true in the context of romantic desire. Cole writes to say farewell to Boris and describes how he's only left with the memory of the departed lover. He says farewell and it is a recollection of previous farewells, an addition to the growing sense that every time they say goodbye will be the last time.

Edward and Gaveston begin to dance, and we come to realize that the music is actually being sung in the past, linking listeners in the present day to the listeners in the past. The song collapses time. The tune is from the 1940s, but it can describe the love between two men during the early fourteenth century, especially given the way that relationship is described by a queer playwright in the late sixteenth century. The film suggests, just as *Red Hot + Blue* does, that Porter's music (written in the middle of the twentieth century) can speak to the time of the audience's viewing (the early nineties, the height of the HIV epidemic), and it even suggests that his music can speak to an even longer history of same-sex affection.

The camera then pans out, giving us the whole scene in deep focus. It turns out that Lennox has been there all along. She has been singing for the parting lovers the entire time, and they pause from their dancing briefly to watch her sing.

And then we have that refrain one final time: "Every time we say goodbye."

The lyrics celebrate how happy the singer is in the company of the beloved, but suffering horribly whenever the two are separated. The speaker likens her mood shifts as being "from major to minor," while the instrumentation of that line begins with an A♭ major chord and ends with an A♭ minor one. It's about tying the music's mood to what's described in the lyrics. But it's also about the stories we tell ourselves about how quickly things can change. As we saw in the discussions through this book, not all the themes of the songs on *Red Hot + Blue* speak directly to issues in the HIV/AIDS epidemic. But "Every Time We Say Goodbye" certainly does. It is a song about two people saying farewell. That is one way to read the "we" in the title and the refrains of the song. We're overhearing the thoughts of a couple in love. But another way to understand the song is that the "we" is us, all of us, we, the living. And it works so well for this scene in Jarman's film.

Longing. Separation. A disapproving society. That's the stuff of Cole Porter's songs and his life, as we have seen. His affairs and times apart from his male lovers, as well as his love and separation from his wife Linda, too, might be captured in this song. But what "Every Time We Say Goodbye" really captures is the way that even small events can take on larger meanings. How must it have been for Porter, after his legs were crushed in the horse-riding accident, to receive visits from friends and lovers? He'd be in chronic, excruciating pain and largely unable to travel. He'd only see visitors for brief periods of time when they come to his home before they'd leave him as he returns to the private confines of the house, his bed or the workspace of the piano. On June 15, 1944, he writes to Barclift and says,

> I'm so sick of having wonderful kids like yourself saying goodbye & disappearing for so long. [...] Every Sunday lunch here now is a farewell party & in spite of the laughs, the under-current here is sad as hell.[10]

Largely homebound, Porter would produce incredible amounts of music but must have experienced so much emotion, too. Here, in his letter to Barclift, a simple goodbye becomes a memory of what's been lost and a foretaste of what might never come again. Life outside the social circle becomes a purgatory of waiting for dreamt-of reunion.

These sentiments in the letters find poignant expression in Lennox's Lachman-directed music video, which was the final one shown in the television special. It doesn't relate so directly to gay rights or AIDS, at least not at first. Instead, we see her watching splices of old home video of a family with young children. She's watching them on one of those old film projectors, sometimes sitting in a chair and other times standing with the images projected partly on her face and partly on the screen behind her (Figure 7.1). So, she's there but she's not there. A young boy and his sister chase after a ball on the lawn, swim in the ocean, and laugh with their parents.

The music video doesn't reveal this, but these snippets are from home movies of the Jarman family when Derek

Figure 7.1 Annie Lennox, "Every Time We Say Goodbye" (*Red Hot + Blue*) (Dir. Ed Lachman, Chrysalis Records, 1990), screenshot from the music video.

was growing up in England in the 1940s. These celluloid memories call back to the child who Jarman was before he knew about romantic love, about heartache, about infection, about how many times he would have to say goodbye. As one commentator puts it, the home movies in the video spotlight "the very fact of AIDS that stains the present with that sense of future loss."[11] These images tantalize us with the notion that one can go backwards in time, that memory is a way to undo the past, or at least that reverie allows us to forget briefly about the perils of the present. Yet even childhood senses of loss—in games, in pretend, in simple things—are forerunners of later loss and numerous times of goodbyes.

Lennox's "Every Time We Say Goodbye" resuscitates Cole Porter's jazz standard in a way that makes the song speak so directly to the emotional weight of the HIV epidemic, even if it was written in a different time. And, in turn, both the video and the song become haunted by the shadow of the epidemic. The young child we see could not have known about AIDS nor could he have known he would contract the disease. Forty years later, Jarman appears as a memory in the very music video he'd be too sick to direct. The film of *Edward II*, too, was impacted by the director's health. He had contracted AIDS-related pneumonia and worked on the film during his homebound recovery. In his diaries, he wrote, "I'm up, and off the oxygen, though still breathless. I spend the morning working on the script for *Edward II*."[12] Jarman would die only a few years after making the film. "Every Time We Say Goodbye" was written at a time when millions were separated from their beloveds because of war. There's that repeated theme, which links this song to so many others on *Red Hot + Blue,* that love is subtended to the constant threat of loss.

In its new contexts, "Every Time We Say Goodbye" takes on deeper meanings as it invites listeners to think about the past in a new way, to connect more closely to the urgency of the present, and to think about what the future may bring. Lennox's music video opens with a statement by the artist. She looks directly at the camera and says, "The more cases of HIV infection we can prevent now, the fewer cases of AIDS will be seen in the future."[13] It suggests that what we are about to see—the homage to Cole Porter, to Derek Jarman, and to saying goodbye—will invite us to treat the past, with all its innocence and all its perils, as the raw material from which we might shape the future.

Notes

1. William Shakespeare, *Hamlet*, ed. Barbara Mowat and Paul Werstine (New York: Simon and Schuster, 2012), 1.1.191–7.

2. "[September 11, 1925]: Cole Porter to Boris Kochno," *Letters,* 56–7.

3. "[September 16, 1925]: Cole Porter to Boris Kochno," *Letters,* 60.

4. "[September 20, 1925]: Cole Porter to Boris Kochno," *Letters,* 63.

5. "[undated] Cole Porter to Boris Kochno," *Letters,* 68.

6. Qtd. in Cole Porter, *The Letters of Cole Porter*, ed. Cliff Eisen and Dominic McHugh (New Haven: Yale University Press, 2019), 71.

7. "Music Icon Annie Lennox Belts Songs of Christmas Love," *National Public Radio* (December 23, 2010).

8. For a discussion of the video in a different context, see John S. Garrison, *The Pleasures of Memory in Shakespeare's Sonnets* (Oxford: Oxford University Press, 2024), 174–7. Some of the writing here draws from that earlier thinking.

9. Arthur Schopenhauer, *Studies in Pessimism*, trans. T. Bailey Saunders (Whitefish, MT: Kessinger Publishing, 2010), 65.

10. Cole Porter, *The Letters of Cole Porter*, ed. Cliff Eisen and Dominic McHugh, "15 June [1944] Cole Porter to Nelson Barclift" (New Haven: Yale University Press, 2019), 199.

11. Katherine Bergeron, "Uncovering Cole," *Repercussions* 4.2 (1995): 28.

12. Derek Jarman, *Modern Nature* (Minneapolis: University of Minnesota Press, 2009), 293.

13. Lennox is not the only artist to connect the song to a current pandemic. As a eulogy to all those lost to the coronavirus pandemic, jazz recording artist Ann Hampton Callaway gave a stirring performance of the song from her home during the period of Covid-19 lockdown.

Coda: The AIDS Epidemic
and Red Hot Today

Through this book, my aim has been to locate us back in the moment into which *Red Hot + Blue* emerged. This mental time travel combines the active work of both forgetting and remembering. In some ways, we live in a vastly different world than the one in 1990, at least in terms of the role of the virus in many people's lives and in terms of a shared social reticence to discuss sexuality. We need to forget how the world is now to reconnect (or connect for the first time) with that period when the HIV/AIDS epidemic was soaring toward its height. Yet it's important to note that AIDS remains a serious public health threat today, and certainly the world has a long way to go in terms of embracing people who might be different from the mainstream.

AIDS is a global health crisis. It's a disease that has become manageable only for those people living in countries where there is widespread access to medications. Even among those people living in more wealthy countries, not all of them have access to healthcare. According to UNAIDS, approximately 40.4 million people have died from AIDS-related illnesses since the inception of the epidemic, and about 630,000 people died from AIDS-related illnesses in 2022. About 1.3 million people became newly infected with HIV in 2022, though new infections have been reduced by 59 percent since the peak in 1995. Globally, median HIV prevalence still remains significantly higher among disenfranchised populations (commercial sex workers, incarcerated people, and injection drug users). About 7.7 percent of gay men (and other men who have sex with men) and 10.3 percent of transgender people are HIV positive.[1] These statistics testify to the continued need for prevention programs as well as access to treatment for the disease. And those alarming numbers among sexual minorities signal there is much work to be done to create a world where people can speak openly about the body and its diverse desires.

So the work continues.

The Red Hot organization has worked ceaselessly to galvanize the music industry in response to that crisis. The success of *Red Hot + Blue* has led to a series of albums from the organization in the widest possible variety of musical styles. The organization's second project was *Red Hot + Dance*, a 1992 album aimed at a younger, club-going audience. Among the tracks was George Michael's "Too Funky," which became a major hit in both the UK and the United States. Madonna also contributed "Supernatural," allowing both artists notably absent from the first album to support the ongoing project. The 1990s continued to bring success for the Red Hot series, with major artists taking the lead on albums in order to rally other performers to the albums and to raise the visibility. For example, Kathy Mattea and Randy Scruggs drew an impressive roster to *Red Hot + Country* (1994). Co-curated by Earle Sebastian and John Carlin, *Stolen Moments: Red Hot + Cool* (1994) combined jazz and hip-hop, garnering recognition as *Time* magazine's album of the year. Red Hot also started releasing albums without the name in the title with *No Alternative,* which was a who's who of alternative rock including Nirvana, The Beastie Boys, Patti Smith, and many others. In turn, this led to the seminal Indie Rock compilation, *Dark Was the Night*, produced with Aaron Dessner and Bryce Dessner in 2009. It also marked the second of several collaborations with MTV, which aired the special and related public service announcements throughout the 1990s.

As I have discussed in this book, *Red Hot + Blue* was both groundbreaking and time-defying. It proved that classic songs could surprisingly speak to a very different cultural context. Simultaneously, the artists' updated versions brought a new perspective on the previous era. Red Hot projects have continued to bring artists of the past in dialogue with the health crisis in the present. *Red Hot + Cool,* for instance, contained tracks inspired by John Coltrane and his "Impulse!" label. *Red Hot + Rhapsody* (1998) paid tribute to Gershwin, while *Red Hot + Indigo* (2001) paid tribute to Duke Ellington. In another move that intertwined past and present to draw attention to the AIDS epidemic, *Master Mix: Red Hot + Arthur Russell* (2014) resuscitated the music of the underground artist who died from AIDS-related causes in

1992. Other compilations have re-imagined works by Bach, Sun-Ra, and The Grateful Dead.

As it grows, the organization has placed increased energy in showcasing international artists and raising awareness about the global reach of the disease. Beco Dranoff led several *Red Hot + Rio* (1996) projects that turned attention to music from Brazil and broader Latin America, including *Silencio=Muerte: Red Hot + Latin* (1997) and *Onda Sonora: Red Hot + Lisbon. Red Hot + Fela* (2013) raised awareness about HIV/AIDS in sub-Saharan Africa. The organization also moved beyond the album model to digital downloads as the market changed, and it has created such non-musical projects as a documentary about AIDS in Africa and a documentary about the Beat Generation for The Whitney Museum of American Art.

There are now more than twenty albums in the Red Hot discography, which showcases more than 500 artists. Its roster includes major artists in the western mainstream as well as artists from around the world. The organization also hosts events such as concerts and danceathons. Its most recent music projects have included recordings to support marriage equality in Southeast Asia, and a forthcoming album celebrates the trans/non-binary communities and features a series of duets between a cisgendered performer and a trans performer. Since its inception, the organization has given away more than $15 million for AIDS-related causes, including the only major outside grant to ACT UP (roughly a million in the early 1990s) and the founding grant to TAG (Treatment Action Group). However, the organization has always been more about raising awareness than about raising funds, and it's found that music is the ideal vehicle not just to move people but to energize a movement with *Red Hot + Blue* standing as its inspiring foundation.

Note

1. The statistics in this paragraph are drawn from UNAIDS, "Global HIV & AIDS Statistics—Fact Sheet," Accessed June 24, 2023. https://www.unaids.org/en/resources/fact-sheet

Also Available

122. *The Pharcyde's Bizarre Ride II the Pharcyde* by Andrew Barker
123. *Arcade Fire's The Suburbs* by Eric Eidelstein
124. *Bob Mould's Workbook* by Walter Biggins and Daniel Couch
125. *Camp Lo's Uptown Saturday Night* by Patrick Rivers and Will Fulton
126. *The Raincoats' The Raincoats* by Jenn Pelly
127. *Björk's Homogenic* by Emily Mackay
128. *Merle Haggard's Okie from Muskogee* by Rachel Lee Rubin
129. *Fugazi's In on the Kill Taker* by Joe Gross
130. *Jawbreaker's 24 Hour Revenge Therapy* by Ronen Givony
131. *Lou Reed's Transformer* by Ezra Furman
132. *Siouxsie and the Banshees' Peepshow* by Samantha Bennett
133. *Drive-By Truckers' Southern Rock Opera* by Rien Fertel
134. *dc Talk's Jesus Freak* by Will Stockton and D. Gilson
135. *Tori Amos's Boys for Pele* by Amy Gentry
136. *Odetta's One Grain of Sand* by Matthew Frye Jacobson
137. *Manic Street Preachers' The Holy Bible* by David Evans
138. *The Shangri-Las' Golden Hits of the Shangri-Las* by Ada Wolin
139. *Tom Petty's Southern Accents* by Michael Washburn
140. *Massive Attack's Blue Lines* by Ian Bourland
141. *Wendy Carlos's Switched-On Bach* by Roshanak Kheshti
142. *The Wild Tchoupitoulas' The Wild Tchoupitoulas* by Bryan Wagner
143. *David Bowie's Diamond Dogs* by Glenn Hendler
144. *D'Angelo's Voodoo* by Faith A. Pennick
145. *Judy Garland's Judy at Carnegie Hall* by Manuel Betancourt
146. *Elton John's Blue Moves* by Matthew Restall
147. *Various Artists' I'm Your Fan: The Songs of Leonard Cohen* by Ray Padgett
148. *Janet Jackson's The Velvet Rope* by Ayanna Dozier
149. *Suicide's Suicide* by Andi Coulter
150. *Elvis Presley's From Elvis in Memphis* by Eric Wolfson
151. *Nick Cave and the Bad Seeds' Murder Ballads* by Santi Elijah Holley
152. *24 Carat Black's Ghetto: Misfortune's Wealth* by Zach Schonfeld